UITGAVEN VAN HET
NEDERLANDS HISTORISCH-ARCHAEOLOGISCH INSTITUUT TE İSTANBUL

Publications de l'Institut historique et archéologique de Stamboul

sous la direction de
A.A. KAMPMAN et Machteld J. MELLINK

XX

THE METAPHYSICS OF CREATED BEING ACCORDING TO ABÛ L-HUDHAYL AL-'ALLÂF

GREGORII MEMORIAE

THE METAPHYSICS OF CREATED BEING ACCORDING TO ABÛ L-HUDHAYL AL-'ALLÂF

A Philosophical Study of the Earliest Kalâm

by

RICHARD M. FRANK

Professor of Semitic Languages
at the Catholic University of America

İSTANBUL
NEDERLANDS HISTORISCH-ARCHAEOLOGISCH INSTITUUT
IN HET NABIJE OOSTEN
1966

Printed in Belgium

TABLE OF CONTENTS

ABBREVIATIONS

abû Rašîd al-Nîsâbûrî, *K. al Masâ'il*	=	Biram, Arthur, *die Atomistische Substanzlehre aus dem Buch der Streitfragen*, Berlin, 1902
Baqillânî, *Tamhîd*	=	*al-Tamhîd fî l-radd ʿalà l-mulḥida wal-muʿtazila*, ed. M. Khodeiri and M. abû Rîda, Cairo, 1367/1849
Farq	=	ʿAbd al-Qâhir al-Baġdâdî, *al-Farq bayn al-firaq*, ed. M. al-Kawthari, Cairo, 1367/1948
Fiṣal	=	Ibn Ḥazm, *K. al-Fiṣal wal-Milal*, 5 vol's, Cairo, 1320
Gardet and Anawati, *Introduction*	=	*Introduction à la théologie musulmane*, Paris, 1948
Ibn Taymîya, *Muwâfaqa*	=	*Muwâfaqa ṣaḥîḥ al-manqûl li-ṣarîḥ al-maʿqûl*, ed. M. ʿAbdalḥamîd and M. Faqî, 2 vol's, Cairo, 1370/1951
Intiṣâr	=	abû l-Ḥusayn al-Khayyât, *K. al-Intiṣâr wal-radd ʿalà Ibn al-Rawândî l-mulḥid*, republished and translated by A. Nader, Beyrouth, 1957
Maq.	=	al-'Ašʿarî, *Maqâlât al-'Islâmîyîn*, ed. H. Ritter, Istanbul, 1929-30
Milal	=	al-Šahrastânî, *K. al-Milal wal-Niḥal*, ed. M. Badrân, 2 vol's, Cairo, 1327/1910-1375/1955
Nader, *Système*	=	A. Nader, *le Système philosophique des Muʿtazila*, Beyrouth, 1956
Nihâya	=	al-Šahrastânî, *Nihâyat al-'iqdâm fî ʿilm al-kalâm*, ed. A. Guillaume, Oxford, 1934
Pines, *Beitrage*	=	S. Pines, *Beiträge zur islamischen Atomenlehre* Berlin, 1936
Pretzl, *Atomenlehre*	=	Otto Pretzl, « die frühislamische Atomenlehre, » der Islam, 19 (1931), pp. 117-130
Pretzl, *Attributenlehre*	=	*die frühislamische Attributenlehre* (Sitzbr. d. bayrischen Akad. d. Wiss., phil.-hist. Abteilung, 1940, 4) München, 1940

Razî, *K. al-'Arba'în*	=	Fakhruddîn al-Râzî, *K. al-'Arba'in fî' Usûl al-dîn*, Hyderabad, 1353
Râzî, *I'tiqâdât*	=	, *I'tiqâdât firaq al-muslimîn wal-mušrikîn*, ed. A. al-Naššâr, Cairo, 1356/1938
Râzî, *Muḥaṣṣal*	=	, *Muḥaṣṣal 'afkâr al-mutaqaddimîn wal-muta'aḫḫirîn*, Cairo, 1323
Šarḥ al-Mawâqif	=	Ğurğânî, *Šarḥ al-Mawâqif*, ed. M. al-Na'sânî, 8 vol's, Cairo, 1325/1907
Tabṣîr	=	abû l-Muẓaffar al-Isfarâ'înî, *al-Tabṣîr fî l-dîn*, ed. M. al-Kawthari, Cairo, 1359/1940
Taftazânî	=	Sa'duddîn al-Taftazânî, *Šarḥ al-'aqâ'id al-nasafîya*, Cairo (Dâr 'Iḥyâ' al-Kutub al-'Arabîya, no date).
'Uṣûl	=	'Abd al-Qâhir al-Bağdâdî, *K. 'Uṣûl al-dîn*, Istanbul, 1346-1928

I. INTRODUCTION

Certainly one need make no apologies in justification of a study of abû l-Hudhayl al-ʿAllâf [1]. My purpose in this work, however, is somewhat broader than simply that of giving a detailed account or a synthetic doxography of his opinions on the 'questions' concerning creation, created being, and created beings, which were under so hot debate among various muʿtazilî authors in the 9th century. There are several more fundamental matters which must be studied before the significance and the meaning of a given author's thought and his particular views on a set of disputed questions can be evaluated and situated within the diversity of the whole muʿtazilî movement during its first phase, through abû ʿAlî al-Ǧubbâ'î and before the kalâm's great bifurcation into the traditions which bear the names of his son, abû Hâšim and of his pupil, al-'Ašʿarî. We must first gain some basic understanding of and sympathy with the universe which they sought to explain. What I shall try to do therefore is to give a description of this universe as it is seen through the system of abû l-Hudhayl.

First and above all we must understand, insofar as is possible across a great cultural and chronological chasm, the meaning which the author is trying to express, — the meaning of which the formulae are the formulation. We must try somehow to recapture for ourselves, out of the texts, something of the comprehension, the *lógos* of the world which expressed itself in this particular form and to restate for ourselves what the author meant to say. Indeed, if, beyond its undoubted social and political significance in the history of Islam, the earlier kalâm was more than a *vanitas et cura superflua*, that is, if it represents a really serious and meaningful attempt of the human mind to understand the ultimate structure of being, it constitutes a 'new thing', an epochal moment in the history of human thought, and is deserving of our most serious consideration. To understand it on this level however, we must see the world through it; that is, in order to understand the meaning of the kalâm and the significance of its statements about reality and the world as an historically defined expression of a genuine human experience of the world, we must somehow grasp the context of potential meaning from within which these statements arose and according to which intended that meaning which is theirs.

---

1 For information concerning abû l-Hudhayl's life, etc., the reader may be refered generally to Nyberg's article on him in *EI*².

More than a few scholars, have taken the attitude that the early kalâm represents little more than a puerile and inept effort to defend the dogma of the *Koran*, that it is nothing more than a polemic apologetic, aggravated by certain differences of opinion on the part of the writers, for the dogmatic content of the Islamic revelation. But such an attitude assumes a kind of bad faith on the part of the authors; it presupposes that even from the beginning there is a complete disjunction between the data of faith and the data of reflective experience and that the mutakallimîn set about to 'defend' the literal content of the former without honestly taking the latter into consideration. Yet such an assumption of bad faith is ultimately simplistic. It does not ask whence and how comes the understanding of the content of the revelation. One may always, after all, whether explicitly or not, say *distinguo* and, at the beginning, the meaning of the *Koran* had itself to be made explicit and defined. In the time of abû l-Hudhayl Islamic dogma had not yet become formally defined in any area. Rather, it was taking form, beginning to take on the definitive configuration of its peculiar character in and among a number of diverse sciences, each of which was to form its own sub-traditions and make its particular contribution to the elaboration of this dogma.

Although from the outset the *Koran* was assumed by the faith of the believer to be the intelligible paradigm through which all being and meaning was revealed and to be known, its meaning had yet to be "worked out;" the exegesis of that meaning which it was felt to make manifest and to render intelligible in the general experience of the community (or that of a particular group, for Islam as a socio-cultural entity was already extremely complex) had yet to be made explicit in thematic understanding and defined [2]. Within such a situation the believer can only come to grasp the meaning of the *Koran* simultaneously with and in the understanding of the world of which he takes it to be the paradigm. Its potentiality of meaning for the believer — its potentiality to give meaning to human existence — is to be discovered within the horizons of a more general hermeneutic situation; since he understands it as a paradigm only within his total experience of the world, his understanding of the sense of the revelation

---

[2] I do not intend to enter here into the broader question of the place and rôle of the kalâm alongside of and in opposition to the other active disciplines (fiqh, ḥadîth, falsafa, etc.) which contributed to Islam's cultural self-elaboration as each, variously influenced by the others, in the common milieu made its own contribution to the evolution of the total tradition; nor, again, would I wish to exaggerate the place of the kalâm in the overall context of the growth of the Islamic tradition, for Islam was, almost from the beginning, an extremely diversified socio-cultural complex. Rather, abstracting from the complexity of the whole milieu, but remembering that it did form the larger, defining matrix, I should like to focus attention in the following remarks on the single problem of the kalâm as it elaborated, from within and into this matrix, a uniquely islamic metaphysics.

can only be brought forth thematically and made explicit from within the structured framework of a pre-predicative grasp of the totality of the world in which his human experience of the world in general and of the *Koran* in particular are given, simultaneously together. The revelation thus becomes the objectively meaningful paradigm through which the world is understood from within a non-objectified total experience which embraces, within a dialectically structured whole, both the *Koran* and the world. The meaningfulness and validity of the *Koran* as a paradigm had therefore to be first understood and set forth in grasping thematically the meaningful and intelligible coherence of the world which was given to human presence, as it was coherent and intelligible, within the paradigmatic framework of the revelation.

In the early period, when Islam's understanding of the meaning of the *Koran* as the model of the meaning and structure of its own existence had not yet been explicitly formulated and defined according to some kind of concensus of the group, there can be no question of a simple imposition of a dogmatic system upon the world and of the consciously arbitrary invention of a conceptual system which would "save the appearances" of the *Koran*, regardless of what non-sense (i.e., what violation of the lived sense of reality) might be perpetrated. Indeed, such an "apology" would be none at all, but would, on the contrary, constitute the believer's own demonstration to himself of the ultimate invalidity and incoherence of that very paradigm which his faith affirmed to make manifest the coherent meaning of all experience.

What kind of speculative system is the kalâm then? -what sort of an effort of the mind, to achieve what kind of understanding?

Unfortunately we have no statements concerning this matter which are attributable to the earliest muʿtazilî authors. The traditional attacks on speculation as such are of little help, for they represent, not simply rejections of particular conclusions regarding various points of dogma, but more fundamentally deprecate absolutely any attempt to dissolve or analyse the original compactness of the revealed and canonical sources of faith. For them, the purity and depth of faith is gained and maintained only in the immediate comprehending acceptance of its sources, wherein lies the only true knowledge (*ʿilm*), all else being vain opinion (*ẓann*). They can therefore only tell us what a part of the Muslim community knew the kalâm not to be.

Again, it must be remembered that particularly during its first period, what passes under the name of the kalâm was far from a homogeneous whole. The Muʿtazila, from the standpoint of its overall theology, does not in any way form a unified school or manifest a single concensus of teaching on any level; the "five theses" by which it is normally defined as a sect are significant chiefly from the standpoint of the heresiographer. The systems, for example, of abû l-Hudhayl, al-Naẓẓâm, and Mu'ammar are all three fundamentally incompatible with one another in terms of their basic outlook and understanding of the world. Our sources, too, are for the most part highly selective, their interest being all too often concerned with only those doctrines which are peculiar to an author and those in which he departs from some norm of orthodoxy. One must also keep in mind that the center of emphasis no doubt varied with different authors [3]; in the intellectual agitation of the time, the principal aim of some was indeed more speculative and theological than apologetic. Nevertheless, whatever the specific intellectual orientation of a particular author, there can be little doubt that the great majority of the Mu'tazila intended, on one plane or another, to define and validate the truth of Islam with the utmost fidelity to the revelation as they understood it. Nader's assumption of the contrary is untenable [4]. There is no evidence in the available texts which would show on the part of the early mu'tazilî writers anything but an effort to describe God and the universe systematically in conformity with a sincere understanding of the *Koran*. The fact that the individual would take to the discourse of rational understanding to defend and define the basic content of his faith indicates, of course, the presence of an apriori non-"traditionist" attitude already in his unreflected approach to the understanding of the revelation; he feels a need for one reason or another, for whatever explicit motive, to analyse the original compactness of his religious understanding into explicit and systematic formulation but this does not in any way indicate any impurity of his faith or denote a lack of sincerity and intellectual honesty in his effort to give a speculative account of Islam. One cannot "demonstrate" the existence of God or the truth of a particular position regarding human freedom and man's power of efficacious action without in some degree making explicit the underlying metaphysical structure of existence which gives coherence to the terms of the demonstration and according to which consequently it stands as a demonstration. *Per se*, the theological conclusions arrived at through the kalâm need not differ one iota from those of the tradition, though it must, of course, be admitted that formulation is very important; its statement is the ex-pression of a particular mode of understanding and it is at this level that the two diverge. Albeit the effort is to see and verify analytically the order of universal being in its concordance with the revelation, as understood by the particular author, the criterion whereby certainty is guaranteed, (that which is felt to be the ultimate ground of the proof as such) remains always the *Koran*, understood in one way

[3] Gardet and Anawati, *Introduction*, 47.

[4] *Cf. infra*, ch. V, n. 9.

or another within the overall horizon of possible meaning. In this way, abstracting from particular conclusions, the first and irreducible difference between the traditionists and the mutakallimîn concerns their attitude towards the very effort to understand and the possible validity of this effort. But there can be no apology without analysis and if the traditionist would "rationally" defend the meaning of the tradition and discursively establish the validity of the content of his faith according to the understanding of the world which is defined in his comprehension of the tradition, he is forced in some degree to abandon the injunction against analytic "speculation" (*al-ḫawḍ/al-naẓar*) in order to insist on the truth of the revelation precisely in its indissoluble compactness. There is, in fact, some evidence for the beginnings of a more "orthodox" speculation alongside the Mu'tazila prior to the time of al-'Aš'arî [5].

From this standpoint then, the question of the kalâm in differentiation from the tradition is one of the degree or the rigidity with which one adheres to one or the other of the polar extremes and secondarily of the particular theological propositions ascribed to these extremes. To the extent that there could be, in the third century of the Hegira, a systematic speculative description of the structure of the universe which belonged to that central, native core of the islamic tradition, whose most conservative expression realised itself in the work of the traditionists, such a description is that of the earlier kalâm.

Still we must ask what — beyond the immediate, stated aim, which is that of an apologetic — kind of understanding is sought in establishing the theoretical foundations of the apology; what kind of knowledge of the basis of its own validity does it assume possible? What is the order of the truth which it seeks in establishing the foundation of its dogmatic assertions? From the outset it is apparent that the kalâm differs radically from Christian theology, even though this too was ostensibly apologetic in its first beginnings [6]. The kalâm did not seek to penetrate rationally into the mysteries of God and His creation, for that part of Islam which was represented by the earlier kalâm was not, like Christianity, the inheritor of the Greek assumption that human reason, of its own innate powers, could uncover ever more of the truth and render it intelligible through and within its own light nor that there was a truth "naturally" inherent in things and in the order of the world as world; faith did not seek understanding in the sense of a further penetration into what was revealed or hope to uncover the truth and order of created existence according to the light of human intelligence. The importance

---

[5] *Cf.* Schacht, *New Sources for the history of Muhammedan Theology*, Studia Islamica 1 (1953), 33.

[6] *Cf.* Gardet and Anawati, *op. cit.*, 313 and generally *ibid.*, 303ff and Gilson, *l'Esprit de la philosophie médiévale* [2] (Paris, 1948), 17ff.

given to human understanding and the demands of reason varied somewhat, both explicitly and implicitly, from author to author, but the early kalâm as such, though having in some aspects the appearance of a kind of rationalism [7], was not philosophical or theological in the sense formally assigned these terms in Western thought.

The kalâm was nevertheless, no matter how understood, a speculative science and as such its aim was understanding: truth. The question is, in a sense, the nature of the truth sought; it is, so to speak, not ἀλήθεια but rather *al-ḥaqq*. Here we must keep in mind that the *Koran* is a most singular book in a number of respects. Conspicuous among them is that, in the way in which it argues, pleads, and makes its threats and promises, it makes, in a certain sense, a kind of direct appeal, in a great number of passages, to a rational level of understanding. It contains remarkably few archetypal figures which of themselves, as they stand in the text, demand to be understood symbolically or allegorically. Unlike the Old or New Testament, the "history" which the *Koran* contains is not — and cannot be — presented as the constitutive historical past of the community to which the prophet addressed his message; it is not presented in such a way that it must be taken up in understanding as the ordered historical past of the believer in his present faith but rather, events are cited often as almost random examples of faith and disbelief, piety and wickedness, and of how God has dealt with men in the past. Again, the *Koran* gives frequently a very bold and almost conceptually elaborated picture of God's dominion over creation in a form culturally and psychologically little removed from the fundamental, unreflected world-view of a significent part of the milieu of the earliest mutakallimîn.

God "created the heavens and the earth *bil-ḥaqq*; [8]" this *Truth* underlies and permeates all creation. All creation, again, stands as a "token" (*'âya*) or vast complex of innumerable "tokens" of God's omnipotent power and dominion. However, the *Koran*, as His Word addressed to man in human language, revealing and self-revealing, is the only token which explains itself, speaking to the hearer in articulate self-expression; it is ultimately the supreme *'âya* and the key which opens the only sure way to seeing and comprehending the true meaning of every other of God's tokens. It was this, I think, *viz.*, the fact that the *Koran* was its own articulate and self-interpreting token of God's Being and creative omnipotence, which forced itself of itself into his understanding, making all other tokens

---

7 *Cf. infra*, ch II, n. 31 and ch. IV, n. 7.

8 *Koran*, 14.22, 15.85, *et alibi*; *cf.* also the interpretation of this by Ibn Ḥanbal (*Radd 'alà l-zanâdiqa wal-ǧahmîya* [Darulfünun Ilahiyat Fakültesi Mecmuasi, 1927] 321) and al-'Aš'arî (*K. al-Luma'* [ed. McCarthy in *The Theology of al-Ash'ari*, Beyrouth, 1953] §115).

visible and intelligible in its light, that the Prophet took as the *'iʿǧâz* : its being its own compelling, self-sufficient evidence of its own validity and truth. So also the *Koran* remained for Islam, even though the *'iʿǧâz* came to be taken in a literary sense, the paradigmatic *'âya* for the understanding of all Being. It revealed not merely the order of the world and the being of creatures in their createdness but also, as the Word of the source of all Truth and existence, manifested the ultimate truth of creation : the meaning of creation and of the existence of creatures as a relationship to the Creator (*al-Ḥaqq*).

The task of the kalâm then, whether as apologetic or as speculation for its own sake, could neither be to penetrate into the revelation in such wise as to go beyond it and probe the mystery of God (*al-ġayb*) [9] nor to penetrate with the natural light of human reason into creation; the revelation as the expressed Word of God was of itself absolute while on the other hand, creation could have of itself no meaning to yield save its very createdness, the true understanding, of which (*al-ʿilm*) was to be had with certainty only through the revelation. The task, then, was one of seeing reflectively and of systematically understanding the Truth of creation that was revealed paradigmatically in the *Koran* — of discovering analytically and setting forth objectively in formal language the underlying structure of the created world as it manifested the *lógos* revealed in the *Koran*. In this way then, the goal of reason was not independently to uncover and make its own the truth of nature and its own existence [10], for this it already posessed. Rather it was to discover, in the reflective contemplation of reality, the metaphysical structure of being, whose truth was the created manifestation of *the* Truth; it was to comprehend and *verify* out of its own experience of the world, through an analysis of the world, the truth which was already given to its preanalytic understanding, how the revealed paradigm was reflected in material creation, in order to validate thematically the believer's understanding of the revelation. The initial assumption is not basically that the ultimate order of existence is of itself rationally and intelligibly ordered according to the norms of human reason, so that it may be discovered by and in the process of reflective thought, but rather that it manifests the creative Truth of God and that the underlying structure and coherence of this manifestation can be analytically described. This is important, for the kalâm's initial and unreflected attitude towards the kind of truth to be attained and the place of reason in its attainment determined its method as well as its form and content. The place of reason is to bring to rational, systematic expression the truth of the paradigm as trans-

9 Taking *al-ġayb* as the non-present, the non-phenomenal: that aspect of the Creator which remains completely transcendent and which He does not make manifest to man.

10 Contemplation (*θεωρία*) is not valued as such in the kalâm; *cf. infra*, ch. III n. 31.

cendent it underlies the multiple variety of discrete and individual events which make up the world. As was pointed out above, this does not mean in any way at all that there was a rude imposition of a pre-fabricated koranic model of the structure of created being upon the reality given in immediate experience, apart from and despite the "evidence" of such experience.

The necessity to question was not eliminated in the light of the revelation. In a sense, indeed, the revelation makes known that aspect of being which is not given to immediate reflection, *viz.*, its createdness from the point of view of the Creator, while leaving yet to be posed the question of the nature of created being as such, and it is to this that the kalâm had first to address itself, even as an apologetic, in order to make explicit the ground of its theological understanding. The primal question indeed, is that of being-created [11]. To the extent that he consciously puts out to describe the ultimate metaphysical structure of being in general, abû l-Hudhayl, for example, does in fact, albeit without an explicit "question" or philosophical doubt, set forth and attempt to answer the primeval question of all metaphysics: "why does anything at all exist rather than nothing? [12]" The kalâm is in this way an *universalis consideratio de veritate* [13] and by this fact has gone far beyond any simple primitivity or naïveté.

We must not be misled in our appreciation and understanding of the kalâm by its form and vocabulary on the basis of our being "accustomed to regard the Greek way of thinking as obligatory [14]." If there is no abstract term for *being* but rather it is always spoken of as a being-created (*ḫalq*) and the modes of being are the modes of being-created, this is no prima facie evidence of "primitivity" [15] but rather an indication that the central problem was, in fact, that of the nature of created being in its being created. So also we must keep in mind that if one finds no terms in the work of abû l-Hudhayl and the first generations of the Muʿtazila for "essence", such terms were nevertheless available; they were used by al-Kindî and can hardly have been totally unknown to abû l-Hudhayl and his contemporaries. If, then, the mutakallimîn refused them, the refusal must have a significance which is to be sought in the structure of the world of which they

---

11 Significantly there is no word in the earliest kalâm for God's being, for this is transcendent and altogether beyond the grasp of human understanding. *There is no univocal sense of Being.*

12 Martin Heidegger, *Einführung in die Metaphysik*² (Tübingen, 1958), lff, citing Leibniz.

13 St. Thomas Aquinas, *In Metaphysica* III, *lect.* 1, §343, cited by K. Rahner *Geist in Welt*² (München, 1957), 73.

14 Bruno Snell, *The Discovery of the Mind* (Harvard, 1953) introduction, p. 1.

15 It is considered by Pretzl to be so; *Attributenlehre*, 55.

sought to give an account. One does not choose a philosophical or theological terminology as he might a pair of socks. It is formed and taken up in the act of reflective consciousness which poses the question, in the act of posing the question; the possibility of a meaningful answer is given already in the form of the question as it, posed thematically within a total context of possible meaning. Any indifference regarding the terminology can only stand in direct proportion to an indifference of disengagement from the existential demand of the question.

To speak therefore of the "absolutely primitive and unscientific way of thinking of the founders" of the kalâm [16], or to see in the early kalâm an inadequate "compromise between revealed religion and a poorly understood and somewhat naïvely handled pre-aristotelian philosophy [17]," or to find beneath its surface "fragmentary accounts of substance [18]" is to alienate it from itself and to judge it in terms of what it was not and did not mean to be. It is, in short, to demand that the structure and the horizon of the experience of being out of which arose the kalâm, ought to have been other than they were and that it ought to have taken up, or even wanted to take up, more exactly systems of thought which lay somehow in the margins of its past but in such a way that they were not and could not be existentially present to Islam [19].

What I wish to suggest therefore is that the chief problem is one of understanding; first and above all we must grasp philosophically the philosophical content of the kalâm. We must get somehow behind the rethoric of its expression in order to see in and through the formulae the way in which reality revealed itself to a certain historically and culturally determined modality of human presence to the world and to understand its validity as a statement of the truth of human experience. It is only after this has been done that we can begin to make a valid and intelligent appraisal of the kalâm's debt to previous systems of thought and to understand it fully in the history of its own evolution, in itself and in the larger islamic context.

---

16 Pretzl, *Attributenlehre*, 8; *cf. infra* ch IV, n. 8 and ch. II, 46.

17 Nyberg, *'Amr ibn 'Ubeid et Ibn al-Rawendi, deux réprouvés*, in *Classicisme et Déclin culturel dans l'histoire de l'Islam* (Paris, 1957), 131.

18 Fakhry, *Islamic Occasionalism and its Critique by Averroës and Aquinas* (London, 1958), 35; *cf. infra*, ch. IV, n. 5.

19 I cannot here go into the question of the falsafa; it began to reach its full and final form later than the kalâm and, as it developed, its real debt to earlier islamic thought was enormous, much more so than is often allowed. For all its appearances, the lógos of the system of Avicenna, *i.e.*, its most basic orientation in what makes it unique, can only be understood from within the islamic tradition which preceded it, not that of classical antiquity.

Remarkably little has been done towards the study and exposition of the early kalâm as a serious theological and metaphysical system; most of the work has been philological. Pines' *Beiträge zur islamischen Atomenlehre* contains yet the best description of certain aspects of the early kalâm but the scope of the work does not carry it much beyond the exteriority of the formulae and it remains fundamentally a doxography. Again Pretzl in his *Frühislamische Atomenlehre* and later in his *Frühislamische Attributenlehre* attempts with some success to penetrate deeper into the philosophical structure of the kalâm, but his work suffers from his explicit conviction that the early kalâm was absolutely naïve and simplistic and a preoccupation with finding the extra-islamic origins of certain of its elements. More recently Albert Nader has undertaken to study the philosophical and theological content of the mu'tazilî kalâm in his *Système philosophique des Mu'tazila*, a work which covers almost the entire range of mu'tazilî speculation in considerable and excellently documented detail. Finally, Majid Fakhry in the first section of his *Islamic Occasionalism* devotes a special chapter to the "metaphysics of atoms and accidents" but his discussion remains on a doxographic level without his treating the problems philosophically. The most penetrating insights into the meaning and intent of the early kalâm remain, I think, to be found in Massignon's *Passion d'al-Hallaj*, even though the treatment there is highly abbreviated and frequently somewhat gnomic. [20]

What I hope to do therefore in this work is to outline briefly the metaphysics of created being as it is found in the available fragments of the work of abû l-Hudhayl. It is best to deal with a single author since it is only within a unified system that any part of the whole manifests its validity and truth and carries whatever conviction it may have as a coherent vision of the totality. Whatever may have been their verbal agreement on the five theses, we can no more validly describe a single and unified concensus about the fundamental and detailed structure of being in the varied systems of the Mu'tazila than we can lump together the Dominicans, Augustinians, and Franciscans of the middle ages and say simply that "the scholastics say...," for there are between diverse authors, basic and fundamental differences of view which are nigh absolutely incompatible and great cataclysms of speculative thought hang often on a split hair.

The reasons for the choice of abû l-Hudhayl are obvious. The Mu'tazilî kalâm was, we must recall, for a century the only developed native theology in Islam and it forms, particularly in the school of Baṣra, the direct forerunner of most of the later kalâm. Allowing then for the typically mu'tazilî theological positions

---

20 There is a work, *Abû l-Hudayl -al-'Allâf* (Cairo, 1369/1949) by 'Alî M. al-Ghurâbî, but it is totally inadequate and needs no further consideration.

and for a number of doctrines which are unique to his thought, even within the Mu'tazila, the work of abû l-Hudhayl stands at the very beginning of what was to become one of the mainstreams of islamic speculation. Certainly a good deal of serious and systematic thought preceded the founding of the great schools of the 9th century. Already in the time of the Caliph 'Abd al-Malik, fragmentary though our information be, we can discern in Ghaylân of Damascus, Ma'bad al-Ğuhanî, Ğa'd ibn Dirham, and perhaps Wâṣil ibn 'Aṭâ' [21] the serious beginnings of later theological speculation, just as one can see beneath the homiletic fragments of al-Ḥasan al-Baṣrî a thorough foundation and outline of much of the thought of al-Muḥâsibî. The real significance and historical influence of the neoplatonist Ğahm b. Ṣafwân has yet to be assessed [22]. The system of abû l-Hudhayl however, remains the first which we can see clearly and it would seem most probable that it was first in his work that the kalâm discovered the form which it sought and began to take on its definitive shape [23]. In his understanding of the metaphysical structure of created being we shall expect therefore to find Islam's earliest complete, systematic account of the universal order of being which it felt to underlie its world. Islam formed the milieu of an historically new and unique experience of being and we should expect to find in the work of abû l-Hudhayl one of the purest and most spontaneous transcriptions of certain aspects of this experience, as it was understood in those circles which sought to understand it analytically. The question of how the world is to be understood is still a question; the problem of understanding had not yet been lost and forgotten in the process of dealing with the already elaborated mechanics of its solution and turned into a debate over the terms of the account rather than the structure of the reality to be accounted for.

To the extent then that we are able to grasp the meaning of abû l-Hudhayl we may hope to gain some insight into the order of potential meaning out of which

---

21 To me it would seem probable that the propaganda of Wâṣil b. 'Aṭâ' was almost entirely political (cf. Watt, *Political attitudes of the Mu'tazila*, JRAS 1963, 52ff and Pellat, *le Milieu Basrien et la formation de Ğâḥiẓ* (Paris, 1953), 176) and the theological theses attributed to him (*e.g.*, *Milal*, 84ff) may in great part be simply the projection of mu'tazilî doctrine back upon the quasi eponymous founder. We have no clear cause to speak of abû l-Hudhayl's having a "theology inherited from the school of Wâṣil" (Nyberg, art. *abû l-Hudhayl* in *EI*²) for the background is certainly more complex than this; *cf.* n. 23.

22 Cf. R.M. Frank, *The neoplatonism of Ğahm b. Ṣafwân*, le Muséon, 78, (1965), pp. 395 ff.

23 Nyberg suggests (*E I*² *art. cit.*) that it was abû l-Hudhayl who introduced atomism into islamic theology. Certainly he is the earliest author within the horizon of our present knowledge by whom a thorough atomism is elaborated. In my opinion however, it is too thoroughly articulated in the work of abû l-Hudhayl and too expertly treated in terms of its basic problems to have been original with him; further I cannot agree with Nyberg (*ibid.*) that he was naïve as a thinker.

the kalâm was generated and understand the experience and the truth which it meant to manifest.

I shall here restrict myself insofar as is possible to the metaphysics of the system, avoiding those questions which are purely theological as well as those which concern abû l-Hudhayl's position on the troubles which divided the early Muslim political community. Thus the "five theses" which are commonly used to define the Muʿtazila, viz., the Unity of God (*al-tawḥîd*), God's Justice (*al-ʿadl*), the promise and the threat of punishment and reward in the next life (*al-waʿd wal-waʿîd*), the "intermediate position" (*al-manzila bayn al-manzilatayn*), and the obligation to fraternal correction (*al-'amr bil-maʿrûf wal-nahy ʿan al-munkar*) will not be treated at all. So also the question of the createdness of the *Koran* will be omitted and, finally, that of man's power to effect his own acts (*al-qudra*) will be considered, not in terms of God's justice, but only insofar as it constitutes a determinative element in the stucture of human existence and forms a point of indetermination in creation.

In the discussion of the texts I have tried to avoid logical abstractions and such terms as "essence" which are basically foreign to the system, hoping to maintain the focus, like that of the author, as concrete as possible. Wherever practical within the limits of clarity and English usage I have tried to retain the author's terminology. Thus "thing" (*šay'*) has been used in almost all places instead of "being" (*ens/Seiendes*) and the term "substance" rigorously avoided, since it carries, out of its history in Western philosophical thought, a whole set of connotations which have no place in abû l-Hudhayl's thought. "Accident" I have retained to render *ʿaraḍ*, always in quotation marks, since I could find no really suitable term in English.

Allâh al-Mustaʿân

II. THE BEING OF THE CREATED COMPOSITE

A. *The Thing as a Composite*

The things that make up the created world are corporeal bodies which are ultimately composed of "atoms" and their inhering "accidents. [1]" Body exists as such through the creation of the "accidents" of composition (*ta'lîf*), juxtaposition (*iǧtimâ'*), contiguity (*mumâssa*), and conjunction (*muǧâma'a*) in the "atoms". It has its specific configuration as being such a body and in being that particular body which it is, with its particular attributes and accidents, through God's creation in its "atoms" of those specific "accidents" of composition, etc., as they are determined in the individual instance, together with such other "accidents" as determine and define every particular property, attribute, and state which may qualify the being of the thing at a given moment. In the composite, each "accident" inheres separately in the individual "atoms," as many as may belong to it [2]. The reality of the thing, then, in its being what it is, consists in the presence (*wuǧûd*) of the total complex of its separate "accidents" in their inherence in the atoms" which belong to it, as their substrate.

The unity of the thing, therefore, in its being that thing which it is, is constituted by its being a body and it is for this reason that "accidents" are said to inhere or to occur (*ḥalla, ḥadaṯa*) in bodies (*'aǧsâm*), although strictly speaking the corporality and the specific configuration of the individual body are themselves the results of the inherence of the created "accidents" of composition, conjunction, etc., in the specific multitude of "indivisible parts" or "atoms" that form the substrate. In this way, the oneness of the thing is that of an agglomerate sum; its basic constitutive units are the "atoms," each with its inherent "accidents," and it is constituted as a unity, in its being a thing, by the mutual adherence together of its "parts" in spatial isolation from and exclusion of others which are

---

1 On the ontology of the composite in the composition of "atoms" and "accidents" *cf, infra* ch. IV. It must constantly be borne in mind that the term "accident" is not here taken in the usual, Aristotelian sense; rather it is a quite distinct concept which is to be understood and defined from within the system.

2 That is, the "accidents" adhere separately in each individual "atom" of the thing, but a single "accident" may, in some cases, belong only to a part of the whole, adhering only, thus, in a particular set of "atoms;" *cf. Maq.*, 319 and 330.

not part of the specific composite. Its oneness consists, thus, in one sense, in its spatial unity alone. From another standpoint however, the unity of the thing in the spatial conjunction of its parts is not a mere conjunction and nothing more, for to the extent that the "composition" which founds the oneness of a particular body is grounded in a unique and separate act of creation which determines it as this body and this thing, its unity in being itself and its distinctness and separation from every other thing is quite absolute [3]. Considered in itself, however, it is a unity of a multitude of discrete parts whose cohesion in forming and determining the thing as a specific thing is founded in the actuality of a particular set of "accidents" which the parts share together, each in its individualty. The thing is thus constituted and defined as a thing, in the wholeness and unity of its being what it is, through the created inherence of a set of specific "accidents" in a particulate substrate. The foundation of its existence in the world (*i.e.*, in space or "place" — *makân*) as that thing which it is, is the composition and conjunction of its "parts" or "atoms" as a body and it is therefore by the thing's being such a body that it is defined. However, although the body, in its spatial, composite unity (the "composition of parts") forms the material ground of the possibility of the being of most other "accidents" in the thing [4], it does not, as such, in any way constitute an intrinsic principle which specifically determines the existence of the particular set of other attributes or "accidents" that may inhere in it [5]. That is, while the composite substrate forms, in the composition of its "atoms," the possibility of the existence of other "accidents," it is not otherwise, in and of itself, the cause of the inherence, in its parts, of any specific set of "accidents," for each "accident" is created by God, in the body, as He wills. There can, thus, be no question of "essences," for there is no intrinsic principle according to which there must exist in a given material body one or another single "accident" or specific complex of "accidents," which, in their total, common inherence in the unified substrate, constitute the total character or nature of a particular existent thing. Although the real presence of certain "accidents" does, in several cases, constitute the immediate possibility of the presence of certain others,

3 This is a separate question which will be treated in ch. V.

4 With several exceptions (*viz.*, movement, rest, contiguity, isolation, and *kawn*) all those "accidents" which may belong to a thing can adhere *only* in a composit substrate, not in a single "atom," (*cf.* references cited *infra*, ch. IV, n. 17); *i.e.*, their being is to inhere in a composit plurality of "atoms" (an extended body) even though they inhere separately in each "atom."

5 In the later kalâm, the "accident" of "being in place" (*taḥayyuz* : the act of being actually existent in a specific location in the world) is taken as the principle of individuation (*cf.* for example abû Rašîd al-Nîsâbûrî, *Kitâb al-Masâ'il*, 6f). For abû l-Hudhayl however, that a thing exist at all is that it exist in a place (i.e., a defined substrate), since it has, in itself, no being at all outside that of its reality in the world (*cf. infra*, esp. ch. V, n. 9). There is, therefore, no question of an "essential" unity of the thing in being that which it is, apart from its actual existence in the world in the spatial unity of its substrate.

one "accident" does not arise from another as a necessary consequent from its principle [6]. Each separate "accident" which contributes to the total being of a thing in its being what it is at a specific moment, is the object of a separate and independent act of creation.

The being of the thing is then that it exist as a specific composit totality, but its existence as such a totality is that it be a sum, created so in each of its elements. It has no essence, nature, or intrinsic principle, by and of itself in its being what it is, that determines the individual qualities and attributes which characterize its being that which it is. It exists, thus, simply as a composite whole (*ǧumla*) of a finite number of discrete elements (the separate "atoms," each with its own compliment of "accidents") to which a given name is applied [7]. In short, the specific attributes and properties which make up its total being, in its being that which it is, have no common principle of their unified inherence together in the thing, other than the creative act of the divine will which made the body a body and the several "accidents" to exist in it.

---

6 There may be several exceptions to this principle, as he would seem to have "length" (*viz.*, extension in space) arise directly as a function or consequent of the "accident" of composition (*cf. infra*, ch. IV, nn. 13f) and to hold that motion and rest are consequent directly upon *kawn* (*cf. infra* ch. II, n. 17). Generally however, each "accident" is considered ontologically separate and independent of every other, forming a distinct and separate object of God's creative power. Thus he says that God may suspend a heavy stone in the air for a period of time "without creating an act of falling or descending" and may conjoin fire and cotton "without there occuring an act of burning" (*Maq.*, 312; *cf.* also *infra*, ch. III, n. 12). In order, thus, to maintain the distinctness and independence of the separate "accidents," abû l-Hudhayl (as well as a number of other early muʿtazilî authors) consistently avoids stating directly that the actual presence (*wuǧûd*) in the thing of one "accident" is the condition of the possibility of the presence of another, but rather reverses the formulation; for example, he says that "it is impossible that God conjoin [in the same substrate] the power of effective action, the act of knowing, the act of willing, and death, just as it is impossible that He conjoin life and death" (*Maq.*, 568). Though he thus, in a way, maintains the logical distinctness of these "accidents" and seeks to affirm their ontological independence of one another, he has nevertheless effectively stated that life is the condition of the existence of *qudra*, etc., given his definition of the contrary as that which exists when its contrary does not (*Maq.*, 376). This is in noteworthy contrast to later formulations which make, for example, life the condition (*šarṭ*) of these "accidents" (*cf.* for example, *'Uṣûl*, 28ff and 105) and represents a radically different view from that which speaks of them as "consequents" (*tawâbiʿ*) of life, as *Šarḥ al-Mawâqif*, 4, 184: وقالت المعتزلة باسرهم توابع الحياة كالعلم والقدرة والارادة وسائر ما يشترط فى قيامه بمحله الحياة (*cf.* also *ibid.* 2, 215).

7 ... الجملة التى وقع عليه اسم (*Maq.*, 329). Names are given to those things (*entia*) which are perceived in their existence as distinct entities, God being the author of perception (*cf. infra* ch III, nn. 11f) and so the guarantor of the reality of the named (*cf.* also the *Koran*, *Sûrat al-'Insân* (76), v. 1 and the remarks of Massignon *Passion*, 549). On the use of *ǧumla* for the whole thing insofar as it is a body, *cf.* also *Farq*, 79: الجزء الذى قامت به الحركة هو المتحرك دون غيره من اجزاء الجملة.

B. *Becoming*

Strictly speaking, abû l-Hudhayl does not recognize becoming or the process of change in the sense in which western thought generally gives these words; *i.e.*, he does not know the *coming-to-be* of a thing out of something which was not it nor admit of alteration or change as a continuous process of becoming, such as the *metabolai* which are treated by Aristotle in *Physics* V or the "motions" (*ḥarakât*) listed by his contemporary, al-Kindî in his *Risâla fî l-ʿilla al-ğarîba lil-kawn wal-fasâd* [8]. However, albeit he does not know the categories of coming-to-be and passing-away in one sense, things do in fact come to be and thereafter undergo change while remaining themselves what they are and this fact the system must and does account for in its own way. The ontology of the becoming of things is one of the foremost problems of the system.

The initial coming-to-be of a thing is "its being made to be or its being created after its not being," God's "initiation of its existence after its non-existence, for the first time [9]." We may thus speak of an absolute coming-to-be as of the total composite of the thing in the initial "composition" of its body, together with such other "accidents" as may simultaneously be created in it. In this same way, we may also speak of the initial creation of the existence of but a single "accident" which "comes to be in the body" (*yaḥduṯu fî l-ğism*), as for example, whiteness or an act of perception on the part of man. In the coming-to-be of the whole composite as in the coming-to-be of a single "accident," considered from one aspect, the cases are ontologically identical, in that they represent, in one case

---

[8] *Cf. Rasâ'il al-Kindî*, ed. M. abû Rîda, 1 (Cairo, 1369/1950), pp. 214ff, in which he treats (pp. 216ff) motions which are مكانية وربوبية واضمحلالية واستحالية. The terms *kawn* and *fasâd* as they are used by al-Kindî and the falâsifa meaning "coming-to-be" and "passing-away" do not occur in abû l-Hudhayl or the other early kalâm authors. Again, where abû l-Hudhayl uses the term "creation" (*ḫalq*) and the "initiation (of existence)" (*ibtidâ'*), al-Kindî uses تهوى (*op. cit.*, 161f) which is possibly derived from Syriac ܐܬܗܘܝ, though the editor (preface, p. 21) considers it to be taken from the pronoun هو (without taking into account that the term هوية is probably in the translations, a transcription of Syriac ܗܘܝܐ; cf R. Frank, *The origin of the Arabic philosophical term* انية, Cahiers de Byrsa, 6 (1956), 188, n. 4). Al-Kindî also uses for this *'ibdâʿ* (*op.cit.*, 165, where it is defined) and *ta'yîs* (*ibid.*, 183). With al-Kindî, as with the falâsifa generally, the concepts are altogether different from those of the kalâm, as he speaks (*ibid.*, 217) of حركة... اما ذاتية وعرضية and of *fasâd* as انتقال عن عينه الى عين اخرى (*ibid.*), where abû l-Hudhayl would use *fanâ'* or *buṭlân*.

[9] *Maq.*, 363f, *et alibi.*

as in the other, the coming-to-be of "accidents" in their being created in the substrate [10].

Abû l-Hudhayl does speak of an "accident" of "becoming" (*kawn*, pl., *'akwân*), wherein he does recognise a kind of continuous process, *viz.*, a defined process of becoming in time and place from "this" to "that." In this sense, it is a specific becoming through time, in space and direction. We must keep in mind however that the objects of God's will are realised simultaneously with the act of His willing [11], so that individual "accidents" are complete and perfect as they are created in the thing at the moment of their creation. Within the system then, the ontological reality and being of a thing, in all the states of its being, whatever successive alterations of state it may undergo, lie not in any continuum of progression or process, marked and measured by the act of a given state, but in the discrete acts of the perfected realisation, through creation, of the "accidents" whose actuality *is* these states. He conceives the succession of states not as moments which the mind notes and designates by name as "points" along a line of continuous becoming but rather the apparent, ontic continuity of being in becoming is a line which the mind plots through the points which are the moments of the realisation of the successive states in the actuality of a succession of ontologically discrete "accidents" in the thing. To this we shall return shortly.

The being of a thing in movement or rest [12] (and so, consequently, also the being of movement and rest as "accidents") does not consist in the duration in being and becoming through and between two points of time in space [13]. Rather, the reality of movement lies in the final and perfect realisation of its "passage" between two particular moments (*waqtân*) in specifically designated points in space, as the reality of "rest" is the perfected actuality of being in the same place in the second moment [14]. *Kawn*, on the other hand, is a "becoming in space"

---

10 On the creation of the "atoms" or the substrate as such, cf. ch. IV.

11 *Maq.*, 418.

12 Diverse types of movement and rest are listed in *Maq.*, 345, 361, *et alibi*.

13 The term "space" of course is not used by the author, nor does the term *ḫalâ'* (the void) occur in any of the fragments. He would, however, seem to conceive of a kind of space as a homogeneous milieu of potential local existence; note that he says (*Maq.*, 323) that a thing may "move from nothing to nothing," for place is defined by the presence of the thing — a single atom or a body in the defined multitude of its atoms.

14 *Cf.* the references cited *infra*, n. 17. Abû l-Hudhayl's conception of time is obscure and one cannot tell to what extent his thought on the subject was elaborated. Like all other created things, time is an "accident" but since it cannot belong to the corporeal being as inherent in it and a part of its reality, it does not occur in any substrate (*Maq.*, 367 and 369), i. e., it is immaterial. (On "accidents" not in substrates, *cf.* also *infra*, ch. V, concerning the act of creation). Time is created by God in discrete

and as such is "distinct from motion, rest, and contiguities;"[15] it is, we might say, the extended moment of being in space, whose reality is the realisation of spatio-temporal directionality, relative to and within two specifically defined limits of before and after and, if movement is involved, of here and there[16]. The act and reality of *kawn*, therefore, as a "becoming in space" is other than the realised act (in abû l-Hudhayl's terminology, "accident") of motion or rest which may be involved in such a becoming, as its term[17]. Within the paradigmatic framework of a universe wherein all being is realised in discrete "quanta," abû l-Hudhayl thus conceives *al-kawn* as the act of being temporally located in space, as this act is distinct from the perfected actuality of movement or rest, etc.[18]

As such then, *al-kawn* is, within its own real termini, a single indivisible act ("accident"), realised in the thing, whose unity is constituted between the spatio-

---

units and "accidents" are divided (*inqasama*) in their being according to the single moments of time (*Maq.*, 319), motion occuring in discrete acts in each time (*waqt, zamân*) (*ibid.*). The sources unfortunately do not furnish us with the information by which its relation to the being of things can be fully analysed.

15 *Cf. Maq.*, 325, 351, and 355; he is no doubt using "contiguity" (*mumâssa*) here to imply also the "accidents" of juxtaposition, separation, etc. Abû l-Hudhayl's position in this differs from that of most other authors, who take *kawn* as a general term embracing motion and rest, etc. (*e.g.*, Naẓẓâm (*Maq.*, 351), Muḥammad b. Šabîb (*ibid.*, 354), al-Ǧubbâ'î (*ibid.*, 352, 355), *et al.*). Later, with both the Mu'tazila and the 'Ašâ'ira, *al-'akwân* is used almost universally to indicate the "accidents" classed under *ḥaraka, sukûn, iǧtimâ'*, and *iftirâq*.

16 Massignon notes (*Passion*, 560) that "'Allâf et 'Ash'arî ont donné une coloration matérialiste, spatialisation, au mot *kawn* en le liant par un nexus à l'atome qui y surgie;" in this he would seem to be taking the word in the wrong sense of "becoming," *viz.*, as a coming to be out of something. At any rate, his equation (*ibid.*) *kawn* = *'ayn* = *makân* (following *Šarḥ al--Mawâqif*, 5, 7ff?) is not applicable to abû l-Hudhayl, albeit he cites him. Much more exact is the statement of Pretzl (*Attributenlehre*, 47) that the *'akwân* are the "Seinsweisen des Dinges im Raum," although here too, since he is discussing the use of the term in the majority of the Mu'tazila, what he has to say is not fully applicable to abû l-Hudhayl. Nader's rendering of *kawn* by the word *génération* (*Système*, 170ff, passim) is misleading.

17 *Cf.* references cited *supra*, n. 15. It is thus that he says (*Maq.*, 325) that "the body, at the moment of God's creating it is كائن لامتحرك ولاساكن (*cf.* also the remarks of Ǧurǧânî and Siyâlkûtî in *Šarḥ al-Mawâqif* 2, 216 and 6, 166 and also *infra*, ch. IV, n. 17). As the term *kawn* is used in the few fragments in which it occurs in context (*cf.* esp. *Maq.*, 237 and 350f) it seems at first somewhat obscure, though if it be taken as I have here defined it, the meaning is clear enough; what he is saying in these two passages is simply that if a man effect, in "the first moment," a *kawn* (*viz.*, an act of spatially oriented becoming) towards the right, the movement, at the instant of its realisation "in the second moment" will be to the right, etc. Al-Baġdâdî, who is not the most perceptive of our sources, says (*'Uṣûl*, 40f) that despite his efforts, abû l-Hudhayl was unable himself to make sense of this distinction between *kawn*, motion, rest, etc.; *cf.* the same kind of polemic, *ibid.*, 92 and 134.

18 *Cf. supra*, n. 6, concerning the ontological separateness of "accidents."

temporal limits which define the indivisible discreteness of its being [19]. As an "accident," although again it is the realisation in the thing of the extension of being-between two points of time in space, it remains in itself ontologically distinct from movement and rest and most importantly, though a kind of becoming in the unity of its being-between its temporal and spatial termini, it is altogether distinct from the existence of the thing as the ground of its reality and from its being in its continuation and perdurance in existence (*al-baqâ'*) [20].

Motion or movement (*al-ḥaraka*) is a created "accident" which "comes to be in a body" or some part of a body [21]. Although movement is a thing's "transference from the first place and its departure from it", [22] it is not a "becoming" (*kawn*), as was noted, but an "accident" which comes to be in the thing as a completion or perfected act of *having moved*. This is not in any way to say that abû l-Hudhayl does not consider the act of a body's passing from one point to another in space as continuous along its path; he expressly rejects any notion of a "quantum leap [23]." The problem is rather that in discussing the "accident" of movement, he is not treating of the fact of traversing a trajectory through space, as this constitutes a continuous event, but of movement as a moment in the being of a thing, which qualifies and defines the thing as being in a place other than that in which it was in the previous instant. That is, the focus of the discussion is on movement in the ontology of the thing as a composite of "accidents" and "atoms" not on motion as a physical event. Thus conceived, movement is *in* the thing, its reality consisting in the perfection of the being of the thing in its being "in the second place" at the first moment of its being there [24]. Movement, thus,

---

19 Concerning the kind of thought which underlies this view of things, cf, the remarks of Henri Bergson *Matter and Memory* (N.Y., Anchor Books, 1959), 203f and *Evolution Créatrice*[86] (Paris, 1959), 303ff; *n.b.* also the remarks of J.P. Sartre on the concept of the "instant," in *l'Etre et le Néant*[55] (Paris, 1957), 544.

20 Cf. *infra*, ch. V.

21 *Maq.*, 321f and *Farq*, 79; since the thing is one in the unity of its body, we say that the thing has moved and the movement is attributed to the whole composit, even though only a part of it may move (*Maq.*, 319); al Baġdâdî (*Farq*, *loc.cit.*), either for polemical reasons or through ignorance, distorts the intention of abû l-Hudhayl in this point.

22 *Maq.*, 355.

23 *Maq.*, 321.

24 The "accident" belongs to the "second moment," for its reality in being is the perfection of its actualisation; thus he says (*Maq.*, 233) : وهو يفعل فى الاول والفعل واقع فى الثانى لان الاول وقت يفعل والثانى وقت فعل (*cf.* also *Milal*, 73f, *Šarḥ al-Mawâqif* 6, 100). This statement should not be dismissed as a simple play on the aspects of the Arabic verb, through some simplistic understanding of the relationship between language and perception.

has its being as a discrete moment ("accident") in the reality of the thing [25]. It can have no perdurance or continuance in existence (*baqâ'*) [26] since it is terminated in its coming to be at the very instant of its actualisation as an "accident," when the thing of which it is the perfection either comes to rest or goes on to a second movement. Thus also a single "atom" may have only a single motion at a time, although a single body may be moved in its several parts simultaneously by more than one agent, in which case we speak of a single movement of the body as a whole [27].

While motion has no duration whatsoever, other "accidents" may endure (*qad tabqà*) through a period of time or, more strictly, over a succession of moments. The body (*ǧism*) may endure through the perdurance of the "accidents" of "composition," etc., together with a number of other "accidents" which determine certain more or less permanent characteristics of its being that thing which it is, *e.g.*, color, life, etc. [28] There is thus, according to abû l-Hudhayl, a real continuity of being in a thing, in the perdurance in existence (*baqâ'*) of a particular set of "accidents" over and through the passing into and out of existence of others. We say that "an 'accident' comes to be in a body" since the body, in its corporeal actuality, remains stable in its existence through the perdurance of the "accident" of composition, which is the basis of its being a body [29] and is modified in the states of its being by the coming to be of a new "accident" and the annihilation of the contrary, which it supplants [30].

In this respect, then, body is conceived as the basic, stable or quasi permanent foundation of the being of things in their real presence in the world and the basis of their continuity of being in their existence. We must remember however that

---

25 Motion, like all other "accidents" which belong to a substrate, "comes to be" (*ḥadaṯa*) in the thing (*Maq.*, 355) and inheres (*ḥalla*) in it (*Maq.*, 319). According to Nader (*Système*, 175ff), abû l-Hudhayl speaks of the "penetration" of motion into the body through the activity of the agent. The expression is not, I think, altogether exact if one takes into account the fact that abû l-Hudhayl is not primarily discussing the physical event in, the same way that he does not mean by *qudra* or *istiṭâ'a*, as "accidents" belonging to man, the mere ability to cause the transfer of physical energy to a material object (*cf. infra*, ch. III, n. 22). Nader's statement (*ibid.*, 177) that, for abû l-Hudhayl, movement is an *écoulement* involves the same misunderstanding.

26 *Maq.*, 358, *et alibi.*

27 *Maq.*, 319; thus he says (*ibid.*) that "accidents" are divided according to time, place, and agent, *i.e.*, that each one is distinct as the product of a single agent (*fâ'il*), inhering in a single "atom" (*cf. supra*), at a particular moment.

28 *Cf. Maq.*, 358f, *Šarḥ al-Mawâqif* 5, 27 and 38f, *'Uṣûl*, 50f.

29 He speaks of *baqâ' al-ǧism*, *Maq.*, *loc. cit.*; on its being in the act of composition (*ta'lîf*), *cf. infra*, ch. IV, 2.

30 *Cf.* his definition of contraries, *Maq.*, 376, *cit. supra*, n.6.

the "body", which constitutes the unity of the thing in its being and its continuity in being in identity with itself, is not "corporality" or an abstract principle of the thing's being, but is always to be understood as the specific, real individual body, qualified by its particular dimensions and configuration and such other enduring "accidents" as may have been brought to actuality in it, while its act of existence and the permanence in existence of whatever enduring "accidents" may belong to it, for so long as each may individually perdure, is grounded in God's act of creation and His further maintaining the several "accidents" in being. That is, the thing, as that which continues in existence, identical with itself, through change, is the created composite of undifferentiated, indivisible parts, in which adheres a given set of enduring "accidents." However, since each "accident" which inheres in the corporeal composite is ontologically distinct and independent of every other in its created inherence, there is no principle intrinsic to the particular complex of "accidents" which formally constitutes the being of the thing in the unity of its being that which it is. Each corporeal thing is ontologically unique in its being a particular agglomerate sum of "accidents," the object of a particular act or series of acts of creation. A thing is, therefore, pragmatically defined or *named* as being a body having such a particular set of attributes [31]. As such, however, things do have a permanence in being and a continuity in their identity with themselves over the successive changes which come to be in them.

The becoming of a thing, as its initial coming-into-existence, is the absolute initiation of its being in an act of creation which has no ontological continuity with any preceding being. On the other hand, its becoming, in the sense of the alteration and change of certain of its particular "accidents" is a kind of progress in the thing of a series of discrete and discontinuous states whose actualisation in being is achieved through the immediate activity of an outside agent in the creation of particular "accidents" and the simultaneous annihilation of their contraries in the thing. In the case of the creation of these "accidents" there is a continuity of being in the thing, nevertheless, with its existence in its previous states, in that each new "accident" does in fact supplant its contrary. In each case, the contrary, in a certain sense, underlies the real possibility of the realisation of a given "accident," so that in their alternate inherence in the composite thing the actualisation of a given "accident" is, in a sense, founded in a potentiality of the thing, represented by its prior state as qualified by the inherence of the contrary

[31] *Cf.* for example, the definition of man, *Maq.*, 329. There is a remarkable similarity to modern biological definitions of species (*viz.*, a list of physical characteristics) and Massignon is quite right in speaking of "un positivisme tranchant, et un matérialisme implicite, (qui) amenaient donc à refuser absolument toute existence aux idées générales." (*Passion*, 553).

"accident [32]." On the other hand, the real potentiality lies in the possibility of an act of creation which in no way is dependent upon the thing, so that strictly speaking we cannot say that the actualisation of a new "accident" arises from a "potency" essentially belonging to the thing in which it comes to inhere. The actualisation of a new "accident" in the thing can only be said to conform to the "nature" or character of the thing in that the act of creation, which was the initiation of its existence as a whole determined it and endowed it with a certain finite complex of "accidents" which thereafter, according to the will of the Creator, form the proximate basis for subsequent change in its being a "body" and in those "accidents" which form its more or less permanent attributes as such and such a thing, together with others which give way to their contraries in the process of change. The "potentiality" of the thing is wholly dependent upon an "arbitrary" act of creation just as the realisation of the new "accident" in the thing depends upon another. The given "accident" is annihilated by the agent which causes the inherence of its contrary [33].

By virtue of its being that which it is, the thing has no intrinsic principle or "nature" (φύσις) by which changes and alterations are originated from within it [34], but rather it exists, in and of itself, only as capable of being changed [35]. It exists in the world as the created locus of the possibility of the realisation of another act of creation. We cannot, in a sense, properly say that it *has* of itself a potentiality but only that it is the possible object of the potentiality of an extrinsic agent — that it is *maqdûr 'alayhi* [36], for the passive potentiality which may be predicated of it has no being save in correlation to the actual power of

---

32 In view of this and considering the ontological place of the body in the total composite, one might be tempted to take the body as "substance," comparing abû l-Hudhayl's statement that "bodies are not contrary to one another" (*Maq.*, 376) with that of Aristotle (*Metaphysics*, 1068a, 10f) that οὐσία has no contrary. This cannot be done, however, for several reasons; most importantly, the formal reality of the thing, according to abû l-Hudhayl, is the "accidents" since, other than "accidents", the thing is not anything. Further, the reasons for which Aristotle holds that οὐσία has no contrary (*cf.* St Thomas Aquinas, *in Meta.* XI, *lect.* xii, §§2378-84) are altogether different from those for which abû l-Hudhayl says that bodies are not contrary to one another. "Accidents" are contrary to one another *per se* (*Maq.*, 359, *et alibi*) and contrary succeeds contrary in the individual parts of the substrate, while body arises through the "accident" of composition (*ta'lîf*) as it inheres in the "atoms" and ceases to be with the annihilation of *ta'lîf* and the creation of the "accident" of disjunction (*iftirâq*) or isolation (*infirâd*) in the individual "atoms." However, *cf. infra* ch. IV, nn. 14 and 21.

33 *I.e.*, the contrary does not itself annihilate its contrary, *Maq.*, 376.

34 Concerning φύσις, *cf.* the remarkable discussion of M. Heidegger, *Einführung in die Metaphysik*, 10ff.

35 Man forms an exception to this; *v. infra*, ch. III.

36 There is no term for passive potentiality as a quality belonging to the thing or as a fact of its existence. *Qudra*, indeed, is used in some contexts in a way seemingly parallel to that of Greek δύναμις as in the statement لان الفعل اذا خرج من القدرة خرج منه ضده بخروجه (*Intiṣâr*, 17), but here, as always, *qudra* is a positive and distinct attribute of the agent who is *qâdir*.

an agent to act upon it; with the absence of a specifically defined potentiality (*qudra*) on the part of an agent which is present to the thing, it has *no* possibility of change [37].

In sum, though there be a real continuity and stability of the thing in its being, through the permanence of certain "accidents" which collectively make up, in the unity of the body, the formal reality of its being, its being in the alteration of states which it may undergo consists ontologically in a "progress" through discrete and discontinuous stages in that one "accident" is altogether annihilated and another created in its place. Since the ontological potentiality and the cause of the actualisation of change in no way reside in any inherent "nature" of the thing, but only in the factic presence of a given complex of specific "accidents," the being of the thing is ontologically complete and perfect at any given moment with the created actuality of the "accidents" that have been realised in it. Becoming, as change, is ontologically a progress through extrinsically determined, discontinuous stages, in each of which the being of the thing is completely and exhaustively realised.

C. *The Finitude of Created Being*

All created being is composite (*ḏû 'ab'âḍ*) according to abû l-Hudhayl, and as such is finite [38], in contrast to God, the Eternal, Who is infinite in the absolute simplicity of His Being [39]. In the composite material creature, we have always to deal with a finite whole or totality (*kull, ǧamî'*), for corporeal being exists, in the unity of the composite, as a finite sum of elements. It has its being as a defined aggregate of discrete, indivisible parts in which inheres a determinate set of distinct "accidents," while each "accident" inheres separately in the individual "atoms," complete and undivided in its actuality. A "being-at-rest" (*sukûn*) may endure two moments, but the act of being at rest is, in itself, as it inheres in the thing, one and undivided in each "atom" in which it inheres and, inhering in the whole, constitutes a single and undivided act in the total composite which is the thing in its unity as a composite. At every level, no matter how considered, the being of the thing is defined and constituted as the unified whole or sum of a multitude of discrete elements. At any given instant its being is complete and perfect in the created actuality of the total sum of its "accidents," and its history, to the extent that we may legitimately speak of such, is the sum of the discrete moments of its existence: the total of those "accidents" that

37 *Cf. infra* concerning the ultimate termination of all change, esp. nn. 42ff.

38 وجب ان يكون المحدث ذا غاية ونهاية وان له كلا وجميعا (*Intiṣâr*, 16); وجدت المحدثات ذات ابعاض وماكان كذلك فواجب ان يكون له كل وجميع (*ibid.*).

39 Cf. *ibid.* and *infra*, ch. III, nn. 45f.

have belonged to it as having been created in the specific body which is the thing, from the moment of God's initiation of its existence. Its entire being, from the beginning to the end, taken at any point, is in every respect the finite sum of a determined multitude of discrete elements. With the exception of man (a matter with which we shall deal in the following section), a thing, in its being, is never in any way more than it is at any given moment of its existence. It has, of itself and by virtue of its being what it is, no inherent principle of change or transcendence towards any state or act beyond the totality of the "accidents" which define the totality of its being in the immediate moment. Whatever potentiality to change it may be considered to have belongs, as was pointed out, properly to the agent who may effect the change and its remaining in existence, beyond the immediate moment, is itself subject to God's causing it to remain.

The indefinite and the infinite have no part in created being [40]. Those things which are are completely defined in the created perfection of their "accidents" at any given instant and if we would speak of the possibility of being as the possibility of continued existence and change in those things which are, or of the initiation of the existence of hitherto non-existent things, or generally of the possibility of the future in the world, then we must speak of the actually existing potentiality (*qudra*) in reference to which the possibles are possible, *viz.*, God's creative power.

Considered in itself, as one with God's being, His Power is infinite [41]; considered, on the other hand, as directed to its objects in creation, it is "limited" by the number and character of those things to which it is actually directed, that is, those which are from eternity determined and defined in His Foreknowledge of what He will create [42]. In this way then, even in the ground of its existence, the possible exists not as an infinite potentiality of creation which shall progressively be defined (whether unto a term or not is not here in question) by its realisation and actualisation nor as the absolute possibility of what God might have willed to create, but only of those particular events which are foreordained, already determined and defined in His foreknowledge. Strictly, therefore, we should not speak of the possible objects of God's creative activity but only of those particular objects which have not yet been realised and those whose alloted time (*'aǧal*) has not yet come [43].

---

40 On the way in which this is true of man, cf. *infra*, ch. III, 3.

41 *Cf. Intiṣâr*, 80; the question of the Divine Attributes is beyond the scope of the present study; generally, cf. *ibid.*, 59; *Maq.*, 165, 177, 484ff, *et alibi, Milal*, 71 etc.

42 *Cf. Maq.*, 163 and the references in the following note.

43 On the general understanding of *al-'aǧal* as determined by God, *cf. Maq.*, 257, *Fiṣal* 3, 84, and *Šarḥ al Mawâqif* 8, 170f; cf. also *infra*, ch. III, n. 39.

For abû l-Hudhayl thus, the being of created things and of all creation exists always and forever as a finite whole : a completed whole in what has been, of what is actually present in the world, or as the defined totality of what shall be brought to existence. There is nothing, in fact, whose being, actual and potential, is not defined as a *whole* (*ğamî‘*, *kull*) in every respect. The possible in general, insofar as it is a real possible, and the totality of all possibles, as all those acts which God will ever create, must form a finite sum, defined in God's foreknowledge [44].

In consistency with his system then, he concludes, though with some hesitency [45], that "everything which shall be will one day be described as having been" and consequently one must affirm, he says, that there is "a finite whole and totality of what has been and what shall be [46]." Any kind of infinitude of created being is unthinkable. There is a fixed, finite limit to the real possibles as determined in God's knowledge, his *maqdûrât*, and so there must come a moment when all the possibles have been realised and there is nothing whatsoever left "in potency." Even God's power and potentiality to create new things, insofar as it is correlative to its object, is exhausted with the completion in creation of the totality of those things which are defined in His knowledge as the real objects of His power [47].

This principle he applies rigorously. That the material world, which we know

---

44 *Cf. Intiṣâr*, 16 and 90f, *Maq.*, 163 and 485.

45 He is said to have given up or repented of his speculation on this topic (though not necessarily to have recanted !); *Intiṣâr*, 16f, 20f and 92.

46 فان قلتم ان كل الاعراض غيركل الاجسام اقررتم بالكل للاجسام والاعراض... فكل ما يكون سيوصف يوما ما بان قدكان... فقد اقررتم بكل لما كان وما يكون (*al-Intiṣâr*, 20; Nader in translating this "vous généraliserez alors pour les corps et pour les accidents..., pour tout ce qui était et ce qui est" has missed the point entirely). It would seem that abû l-Hudhayl was led to this conclusion and to affirm its theological consequents primarily by the logic of his system — the consistency of created being as discrete and finite (*cf. Intiṣâr*, 16f and 20f). The argument that to allow an infinity on one end (*i.e.*, the future) would necessitate positing an infinite past (*Intiṣar*, 18f, *Farq*, 74, *Milal*, 73) takes on a special quality within this particular system. *Cf.* also the argument used by al-Khayyâṭ in his apology for this particular doctrine of abû l-Hudhayl (*Intiṣâr*, 56) that if there were no term to the acts of the blessed they would have then to be rewarded anew on the basis of their actions in paradise (*cf.* also *Farq*, 75); this is important in that it demands, implicitly at least, an existential *Vollendung* to human existence (*cf. infra*).

47 "...because the things which are objects of [God's] power at present have not all come forth into existence, but when all created beings have come forth into existence and not one of them remains unrealised, dependent upon the power (*qudra*) of its maker, it will be impossible to say that the agent of the act is capable (*yaqdur*) of producing another like it since there will be nothing like it in the power [of the agent], all acts having come forth into existence," *Intiṣar*, 20; *cf.* also generally, *ibid.*, 15ff, esp. 17ff.

(*al-dunyâ*), shall come to an end on the Day of Judgement designated in God's design, is common Islamic doctrine. Beyond this however, the acts of the blessed and the damned in the next life also constitute moments in the reality of created being and to put the term of the being of things at the end of the world is to put none at all. Thus, to the scandal of a great number of Muslim thinkers, abû l-Hudhayl insists that there must also be a term to the acts and movements (the "becomings and movements") of the blessed and the damned — a term in which all created being is ultimately consummated [48]. Unlike Ǧahm b. Ṣafwân, he does not say that all created being, and with it thus the pleasures of the blessed and the pains of the damned, will be annihilated [49], but rather all these shall, at a given moment, be commanded by God to "remain." Thus, as even in created things certain "accidents" may endure, their endurance being a single and undivided act, so also the "permanent and fixed remaining" of the actuality and being of those in the next life must constitute a single, perpetual moment of existence wherein they remain [50]. All existence thus finds its *Endung* and *Vollendung* in the divine command in which it terminates. All created existence is summed up in the moment of one eternal act. In this, it should be noted, the being of each individual remains; there is no confusion. Rather, the being of each individual is complete and fulfilled in the totality of his reward or punishment. In a sense, this totality of actuality transcends the momentary completeness of being in the moments of its existence in this world, for in this final moment of "rest," there is not the permanent realisation of merely a single moment but rather of all the possible pleasures and rewards of the blessed and all the possible pains and punishments of the damned [51]. Again, though we have not the explicit texts to determine exactly how he conceived it, we may say that in these pleasures or pains, in each case, was concretised as reward or punishment, God's judgement of the whole earthly life of each individual, so that in a sense this terminal and enduring moment collects, ratifies, and totalises the existence of each individual [52] and in a single act seals for eternity the whole sum of all existence from Adam to the end of the world.

---

48 *Cf. Maq.*, 358f, *'Uṣûl*, 50f, 94, and 238, and the references cited below.

49 He has nevertheless been accused eristically of having said that they will terminate in annihilation (*fanâ'*); *cf.*, for example, *Intiṣâr*, 17ff and *Farq*, 73f.

50 وصاروا فى الجنة باقين بقاء دائما ساكنين سكونا باقيا ثابتا لا يفنى ولا يزول ولا ينفد ولا يبيد (*Intiṣâr*, 17) and كان يزعم ان الجنة والنار ومافيها باقيتان لا تفنيان ولا تبيدان ابدا (*Ibid*, 18) Generally, cf. *ibid.*, 15-21 and 56f, *Maq.*, 163 and 485, *Farq*, 74f, and *Milal*, 73.

51 He insists that there is a perfection, not a stonelike inactivity in this final "remaining" (*Intiṣâr*, 56f) and says (*ibid.*, 17) that "when the blessed arrive at the last of their movements (to which we have affirmed that there is a finite, numerical totality) all pleasures will be summed up in them." (*cf.* also, *ibid.*, 18 and *Farq*, 74).

52 *Cf. Intiṣâr*, 56f and *supra*, n. 46.

III. MAN

A. *General Remarks*

Man, like all other created beings, is a corporeal complex of created "accidents," each of which is separate and distinct from the other and from the body by which the individual is defined [1]. In this way, man is said to have both "soul" (*nafs*) and "spirit" (*rûḥ*) [2] and is described as living (*ḥayy*), though his life is an "accident" identified neither with soul nor spirit [3] and is other than the individual in the totality of his being himself (*ġayruhu*) [4]. So also, he is capable of producing acts through free choice (*qâdir, mustaṭîʿ*) though this capacity (*qudra*, or *istiṭâʿa*) is other than the will (*'irâda*); it does not consist in "bodily health and well-being" [5] and is distinct from life [6] and, like life, is other than the person himself (*ġayruhu*) [7]. Again, he has, as "accidents," five senses, "distinct from the body and the soul [8]" and intelligence or mind (*ʿaql*), a kind of "sense" (*ḥiss*) which is at once its contents and "the capacity for the aquisition of knowledge [9]." However, the senses are "distinct from the body and the soul; the act of perception (*'idrâk*) is an internal

---

1 *Cf.* the definition of man in *Maq.*, 329 and *Fiṣal* 5, 65.

2 The place of both *nafs* and *rûḥ* in the system is obscure, since they are hardly discussed at all in the fragments. *Nafs* is held to be an "accident" (*Fiṣal* 5, 74), distinct from the senses and the body (*Maq.*, 339) and from *rûḥ* (*ibid.*, 337). He says that it may be taken from the body during sleep (*ibid.*, where also *Koran* 39.42 is cited), but does not otherwise, in the available texts, discuss it. It would be important to know if he in any way identified *nafs* with ego consciousness or with the passions (*cf. Koran* 5.33, 50.15, and 12.53). *Rûḥ* likewise "may be taken from him during sleep" (*Maq.*, 337); he is, however, uncertain whether it is a "body" (*i.e.*, a distinct organ and separate complex of "atoms") or an "accident" (*ibid.*, 402) i.e., a function of the body or of a part of the body. From an analysis of human existence as it is construed by abû l-Hudhayl one might, with some justification, question whether *nafs* and *rûḥ* played any really significant rôle within the system; on the other hand it must be acknowledged that our sources are highly selective, being interested only in certain subjects and in these citing often only extreme positions (*i.e.*, those not generally held).

3 *Maq.*, 337; though distinct from life it nevertheless disappears at death by "going out if it is a body or being annihilated if it is an 'accident'" (*Maq.*, 402).

4 *Maq.*, 229.

5 *Ibid.*, and *Milal*, 73f.

6 *Cf.* references cited above.

7 *Maq.*, 229; in a sense the expression *ḥayy mustaṭîʿ* forms a kind of definition, parallel to the *ḥayy nâṭiq* of the falâsifa.

8 *Maq.*, 339; *i.e.*, neither is it a function of the organs of sense nor an act of the "soul."

9 *Maq.*, 480.

act of knowing (*'ilm al-qalb*) which is altogether independent of the physical states of the body and the operations of the organs of sense [11]. It is an act which distinguishes and knows objects and things [12], created directly in the heart by God [13]. Within this, the basis of unity and cohesion being the spatio-temporal cohesion of the "atoms" as a unified body, in which all these diverse and independent "accidents" occur through the will of the Creator, man appears, like other creatures, as a hollow, material aggregate which has no existential unity of interiority and forms no individual, self-centering locus of conscious being in the world [14].

However, though defined as a body having a given configuration in which adheres a complex of distinct and separately created "accidents," man, unlike any other creature [15], has the power of realising his own acts (whether interior or exterior) through conscious choice. To this extent then, he is fundamentally a moral being — one whose being is to produce his own acts and be judged ultimately in his individual and personal responsibility for them. From the standpoint of this investigation, the most important point is that ontologically, in contrast to other created "things," which, as was pointed out above, are in no sense any more than they are, being complete in the finitude of their being at each moment of their existence, man, in being a willing agent (*muḫtâr, mustaṭî'*), has within himself, as a permanent attribute of his being [17], a principle of transcendence : his being insofar as he is *qâdir, mustaṭî'*, is oriented out of the present into the future in the potentiality (*qudra*) of his own acting into the future. We must examine this in some detail, for the thought of abû l-Hudhayl on this point is far from simple.

---

[11] *Maq.*, 569 and 312 (top); perception is "*necessary knowledge*" (*'ilm al-iḍṭirâr*), *ibid.*

[12] *Cf. Maq.*, 361 and further see *infra*, n. 25. There are a number of things involved in this thesis; on the one hand perception and knowledge are distinguished from the states of the body in accordance with the system's general tendency to make all "accidents" separate and independent of one another (*v. supra*); beyond this however, in insisting that the physical states of the organs of sense and the act of perception and knowing (*'ilm*) are totally independent of one another as they take place in the living person, abû l-Hudhayl is, within the limits of his own terminology, saying that the act of perception, as a human act involving a kind of knowing, transcends the mere functioning of any set of organs (the physiologist's electrical discharges, if you will). The completeness with which he separates the two acts, of course, creates other problems.

[13] *Maq.*, 569, 410 and 312. Since man, as the perceiver, does not determine according to his own free choice the content of the act of perception, he cannot be said to be the agent or maker (*fâ'il*) of the act; *cf. infra*. Also involved here is the theological question of the vision (*ru'ya*) of God in the next life.

[14] *Cf.* Massignon, *Passion*, 480f and *infra*.

[15] We have not to do here with angels or *ǧinn*; none of the available texts mention them.

[17] *Cf. infra*, n. 33. The system recognises, it should be noted again, no such thing as an "essential" attribute and *al-istiṭâ'a* disappears finally in the next life; *cf. infra*.

B. *The Structure of the Act*

In the terminology of abû l-Hudhayl, the power of realising an act (*al-qudra*, *al-istiṭâʿa*) is not in any wise simply the inherent power of acting through a release of physical energy on the part of a conscious agent, not the mere availability of raw force to achieve or effect some act. On the contrary, it is the potentiality of effecting a deliberately chosen end; *al-istiṭâʿa* (or *al-qudra*) only *exists* where there is the real possibility of unconstrained choice on the part of a free agent and vice-versa there can be no act of the will (*'irâda*) save where there exists the real potentiality of effecting its object [18]. Any act on the part of man, which is not freely determined in an act of the will is neither his nor, indeed, is its execution said to be wrought by his power of action, but on the contrary must be God's; *i.e.*, involuntary action or inaction on the part of a human agent is not his. It does not arise through any act of his will nor is it realised through his *qudra* but is in every respect God's [19]. In other words, to the extent that action is not a deliberate, unconstrained projection of his own potentiality from within a present situation into the future, man in no wise transcends his momentary state (is not *qâdir*) but rather is moved by external forces through a series of discrete moments in which his being, like that of non-human, material creation, is exhaustively determined, without his intervention and participation as a moral being [20]. Thus, will and *qudra* are what we should term the basic faculties of moral (i.e., properly *human*) action and are accordingly oriented into the future. In man the act of the will and the intention to act always precede the exterior

---

18 *I.e.*, *al-istiṭâʿa* always involves a set of contraries (*ḍiḍḍân*) and the possibility of performing the specific act or leaving it undone; *cf. Intiṣâr*, 17f and 20, and also *infra*, nn. 34 and 37.

19 It is thus that he only ascribes to man those acts the nature (*kayfîya*) of which he understands: كل ما يتولد عن فعله مما يعلم كيفيته فهو فعله *Maq.*, 402; (*cf.* also *ibid.*, 374 and 378, *Milal*, 74 and on the expression *mâ yaʿlam* (*yaʿrif*) *kayfîyatahu*, *cf.* also *'Uṣûl*, 234, which is discussed *infra*, III, n. 51). That event or action whose nature or character is unknown cannot, as such, be intended or willed. Fakhry (*op.cit.*, 44) seems not to have understood this "sublte distinction." N.B., that there is no act or event therefore which is not the direct and immediate result of some willed intention (albeit the secondary *fiʿl mutawallad* on the part of the human agent may in a sense be unintended); the actualisation of the being of a thing (its being brought into being as that thing which it is in the fulness of its being) is primarily attributable only to the agent who knows and intends its being so, to the extent and in so far as he knows and intends it. This notion of a specific, knowing intentionality underlying all events and things is a basic assumption of the kalâm from abû l-Hudhayl through al-Râzî and Šahrastânî, etc., and forms the basis of most of the traditional proofs for the existence of God. Secondary causes are not necessarily excluded in this scheme; rather they are not true or primary causes in that they do not determine the being of the result in a knowing intention which exhausitively embraces its every aspect, as does God.

20 *Cf. Intiṣâr*, 17 (bottom).

actualisation of their object [21]; it is because he conceives *al-qudra* as a potentiality to initiate an event in the world — a nexus between will and action, rather than as simply the raw force or power whereby movement is transmitted to things, that abû l-Hudhayl insists that in the case of exteriorised activity, *qudra* always precedes the realisation of the act [22]. Man's act is *his* and proceeds from his human power to act only to the exent it is the result of a prior intention of the will.

The world and its structure — the perception of things and man's awareness of himself as among and different from them, as the total potential field of action, are given in the act of the intelligence (*ʿaql*), which includes the data of perception and innate knowledge (*ʿilm iḍṭirâr, ʿilm ḍurûrî*) as well as that knowlege which is acquired through thought and reflection (*ʿilm iktisâb, ʿilm iḫtiyâr*) [23]. Given to adult understanding [24] is not merely the raw perception of the phenomenal present but with this is given also the perception of the objective moral good and evil of things [25] and the basis of a natural knowledge of God, together with an

---

21 *Maq.*, 418 *et alibi*; it is unlike God's act of willing, which is simultaneous with the realisation of its object (*ibid.*), for human acts in no way resemble those of the Creator (*Maq.*, 551). Man's internal acts are, however, simultaneous with the act of his will; *cf. Milal*, 73 and *Šarḥ al-Mawâqif* 6,100.

22 *Intiṣâr*, 60f, *Maq.*, 232, *Farq*, 77, *Fiṣal* 3, 22. Human *qudra* does not strictly necessitate its effect (*'awǧaba l-fiʿl*), *Maq.*, 415. Man has, in fact, the power only to initiate motion and rest (*Maq.*, 311f, 350f, 431) and so cannot himself produce or effect, for example, bodily strength (*quwwa*), life, or a corporeal body (*Maq.*, 403; *cf.* also *infra.*, n. 51). It is within this framework that he says that the power to act precedes the act. "Accidents" other than motion and rest result from (*tawallada ʿan*) these, in some instances, and are attributed to the person (*yunsabu 'ilayhi, Intiṣar*, 60) as the one morally responsible while what cannot "result from motion, rest, and the conjunction and disjunction which arise therefrom" (*Maq.*, 311f) but does follow upon the act is produced by God, as for example, the perception and understanding of one's action or discourse on the part of another (*cf. Maq.*, 402, 410 and *Milal*, 74). We need not here go into the detail of the problem of *tawallud* and the physical limits of human action, since that lies beyond the aim of the present considerations; what is here important is that *al-qudra/al-istiṭâʿa* forms, whitin man, the basis of the possibility of effecting his will and so of his moral action in the world. Concerning *tawallud* and the range of man's power to act, besides the above references, *n.b.*, *Intiṣâr*, 122.

23 *Cf.* the references cited above, nn. 9 and 11. Al-Baġdâdî's statement (*Farq*, 78 and *'Uṣûl*, 32) that sense knowledge (*ʿulûm al-ḥawâss*) is, according to abû l-Hudhayl, freely acquired (*ʿilm iḫtiyâr wa-ktisâb*) is to be taken in a different sense if it is not simply contrary to the explicit statement of al-'Ašʿarî.

24 He recognized "stages" in the growth of the mind (in terms of the growth of its contents: its *maʿlûmât* or *ʿulûm*), moral responsibility becoming complete only at maturity (*al-bulûġ*) when the intelligence reached its perfection (*kamâl*), *cf. Maq.*, 480, *Farq*, 78; the broadest implications of all this for revealed and "natural" law (*cf.* the following notes) and the detail of his moral thought I shall not deal with here; on this, cf. *Farq*, *loc.cit.* and *'Uṣûl* 258 and 260.

25 يعلم حسن الحسن وقبح القبيح, *Milal*, 74. Thus it is, since there is objective good and evil perceivable in things, that actions are objectively good or evil and accordingly abû l-Hudhayl speaks of

innate moral demand of conscience that this basis be elaborated in thought and the good persued and evil avoided [26]. Nevertheless, though the world is thus given [27] to present awareness [28] as an objectively structured field of possible action, the act of perception does not of itself contain any appeal to action. That is, the act of perception and understanding, even though containing the objective moral good and evil inherent in the potential of what is perceived, does not of itself transcend the facticity of the given and does not, therefore, constitute for the perceiver an existential situation. Motivation is not given in the act of "knowing," whether in raw perception or reflective consideration, even though the moral potential of the possible actions be given [29]. The factic presence of what is given in perception is constituted as a situation when some possible action (positive or negative) therein occurs to the mind in its immediate potentiality as desirable (*ḫaṭara*), and it is upon the situation as a potential act occuring to the mind that the will must act. The act of perception is created immediately by God so that the presence of consciousness to its own potentiality in the world, like man's material existence in space, belongs to him at any given moment as it is given in the form of a created "accident." Further, the occurance to the mind the of potentiality of the situation as desirable or repugnant in terms of specific acts (*al-ḫâṭir*) is also initiated from without, either by God or by Satan [30]. It is then the givenness of the existential situation, as it presents the immediate possibility of a specific act, that the intelligence (*'aql*) must examine reflectively (*tafakkara*), forming and determining its purpose and intent in terms of moral

unintentional obedience (*ṭâ'a*) or disobedience (*ma'ṣiya*) to God's commands, even on the part of the unbeliever, where there can be no desire of "drawing near to God" (*al-taqarrub 'ilà llâh*); *cf. Intiṣâr* 57ff, *Farq* 75f, and *Milal*, 74f.

26 *Cf. Farq*, 78 and 75f; it is in these terms thus that he is able to speak of a kind of "natural law" (*taklîf qabl wurûd al-sam'*), *cf. Milal*, 74.

27 We shall have, of course, to include in the objectively given the self of the perceiver as it forms, in the state of its givenness at the moment, an object of possible action, as for example the possibility of an interior act (*fi'l-qalb*) — *e.g.*, an act of knowing or of scheming constitutes as possible goal of action.

28 It may be in this sense of the immediate perception of the present (*'idrâk* = *'ilm*) that abû l-Hudhayl said that "acts of knowing (*'ulum*) do not endure" (*Šarḥ al-Mawâqif* 5, 38f); unfortunately, however, while Siyâlkûtî and Čelebî in treating this passage comment (*ibid.*) on this thesis as it is held by the two Ğubbâ'îs, neither gives any further detail or the position of abû l-Hudhayl.

29 This is the clear sense of *Maq.*, 429, 1 - 3 (where the author opposes this position to that of al-Naẓẓâm and Ğa'far b. Ḥarb, who say that there is no perception without a *ḫaṭir*); *cf.* also *Milal*, 84.

30 *Cf. Maq.*, 429 and *'Uṣûl*, 27; as every act is objectively good or bad (*i.e.*, one of obedience or disobedience to the divine law), so also the double source of motivation or inclination, which must be from without. Man is not himself the conscious agent of his own first impulse of attraction or aversion to a given object, nor can things, which neither in themselves nor in their being perceived transcend in any way the givenness of their being at the moment, be the source of an act. *Cf.* also Massignon, *Passion* 492 and *infra*, n. 32.

good and evil which are objectively contained in the elements of the situation [31]. Finally, it is upon the known as given in the product of present perception, prior knowledge, and reflection that the will makes its decision whether to perform the specific act or not [32].

C. *The Being of Man: Givenness and Transcendence*

Man thus as *mustaṭî'*, has the capacity of transcending his own present. However, this freedom of transcendence is highly contingent, although his being is not bounded completely in the finite term of the moment. The fact of his freedom, first, is given him as an inescapable component of the structure of his being; i.e., *al-istiṭâ'a* is given by a divine act of creation so that man cannot choose to be *mustaṭî'* and cannot therefore escape the ultimate judgement of himself in his acts. Again, although *al-istiṭâ'a* is a permanent element ("accident") of his being [33] which covers thus categories of acts, the real possibility of its actualisation is only given within the terms of a specific situation which cannot be willed;

---

31 On the importance of intelligence (*'aql*) in Islamic moral thought, *cf.* Gardet and Anawati, *Introduction*, 347ff; reflection, according to abû l-Hudhayl, does not necessarily produce motivation to the act but elaborates the potentiality of the situation in terms of the given potential so as to establish intent, which becomes the actual motive or intention through the act of the will. Again, though the question of the nature of faith and the ultimate perfection of action in the intended act of obedience to God (*Maq.*, 266f) is a theological question into which we need not enter here, it should be noted in passing that within the general framework of abû l-Hudhayl's thought, contemplation is not valued but rather intellect (*'aql*) is oriented almost totally towards action; *i.e.*, though the highest priority is given to the recognition and knowledge of God (*ma'rifat Allâh*) the place of this knowledge in man's existence is to direct his actions as faith (*cf. Maq., loc.cit*). "This world is a place of action": ان ابا الهذيل يزعم ان الدنيا دار عمل وامر ونهى ومحنة (*Intiṣâr*, 56). πρᾶξις takes complete precedence over θεωρία. Man's self-possession and self-totalisation lies in action not knowing (*cf. infra*). On this world as *dâr 'amal*, *cf.* also the remarks of al-Ḥasan al-Baṣrî in *Hilyat al-'Awliyâ'* (Cairo, 1357-1938) 2, 140 and the remarks on his attitude by Ibn Sîrîn (for whom salvation was by grace alone), *ibid.*, 270.

32 He does not describe the structure of the act of the will; i.e., he does not discuss the actualisation of its decision as a choice in any of the available texts. *Al-ḫâṭir* is clearly not the act of the individual to whom it occurs; it "happens to him" and consequently an external agent must be assigned. On the other hand, by definition, within the system, the act of the will, to the extent that it is a free decision, is preëminently *the* human act. The problem is that the author could not give man an infinite regression of acts of the will and at the same time could not make God the agent, since this would destroy utterly the concept of human freedom. It is for this reason that Ibn Taymîya says (*Muwâfaqa* 1, 206f) that "the Basra school of the qadarî mu'tazila end up having to say that the act of the will on the part of the creature takes place without an agent and so they deny the agent of the act of the will even while affirming that it has a final cause."

33 *Maq.*, 230; cf. also *Intiṣâr*, 61f.

its actuality is entirely contingent upon the givenness of a situation which defines the specific possibility of the act. [34]

As was noted above, man's existence within the situation, his perception of the objective reality of the situation, and his initial reaction to it as a situation (*al-ḫâṭir*) are not subject to his free choice. Human freedom, then, is a freedom only to evaluate the possibility of acting within the determinations of a situation whose objective structure in its presence to consciousness is given. Within these limits of determination, man, in his freedom to determine his own acts, constitutes an element of indetermination in the world. The actuality of *al-istiṭâ'a* precedes the act so that his being in its potentiality of self-determination is an indeterminate to-be-determined in that the actuality of its being within a given moment is the projection of itself into the future: its actuality of itself as potentially acting or not acting [35].

We cannot, therefore, say of man that his being, like that of other created things, is complete and exhausted in the finiteness of its being, what it is at any given moment. Within the system however [36], the range of indetermination which exists in the world in the being of man is quite narrow. Although *al-istiṭâ'a*, in being an "enduring 'accident'," is a general potentiality to act, its actuality arises only within defined situations in immediate reference to a single pair of contraries (*cf.* note 34). His potentiality of transcendence is therefore in no way one of a creative spontaneity but one only of a choice between two alternatives which arise within a defined objective context. Not only is this context exteriorily defined insofar as it is present to the awareness of the human agent, but furthermore the moral potentiality of the context is also preordained and determined independently of the agent, since although the possibility of acting lies within the power of the agent, the good and evil of his potential act lie within the elements of the context. Man's freedom of self-determination in action is thus minimal;

---

34 Since its reality is always limited and determined as the capacity to perform a single particular act or not, it is said to terminate with the first moment of the realisation of the act (تفنى مع اول وجود الفعل *Fiṣal* 3, 22; cf. also *Intiṣâr*, 20).

35 *Cf. Šarḥ al-Mawâqif* 6, 100 and references cited *supra*, n. 22.

36 This is a kind of "extrapolation," for the matter is not discussed directly in any of the fragments. We cannot avoid the question however, especially given the importance of the idea of the total finitude of creation within the system, as it is witnessed by the author's insistence on the ultimate termination of all movement and change. Given his thesis of the discrete finitude of all created being, which has already been outlined, we can determine with relative certainty the general sense of the finitude of human existence as abû l-Hudhayl understands it.

his existence is in no respect one of a creative interiority of spontaneous contingency [37].

Again, consciousness is present to the world and so to its own potentiality as a potentiality to act in the world, in the temporal series of its acts of perception, each of which is a discrete "accident" created by God, complete in itself, and separate from the others. So also the concomittant act of knowing, though it may contain the past as the present reality of a given possibility, is discrete and complete in its own actuality. We have then a transcendence always from one discrete moment, created by God, to another, *viz.*, that of the realisation of the act [38]. Finally, as the individual's general potentiality to act is realised in a series of isolated moments, the series itself is finite and is ultimately exhausted in a terminus (*'ağal*) which is foreordained by God [39], so that we might say that as an enduring attribute of the person, *al-istiṭâʿa* is given him by God who knows from eternity the detail of its eventual actualisation, as a kind of quantum, finite from the outset.

D. *The Unity of the Person*

In the preceding section we have seen that abû l-Hudhayl has elaborated an extremely subtle analysis of the structure of the human act. We must however ask what is and wherein lies the unity of consciousness as the existential unity of the person in his being one and identical with himself. To what extent must we say that for abû l-Hudhayl man is ultimately no more than an "inert carcass," an "aggregate of atoms [40]?"

It must be noted at the outset that in defining man as a material body [41], abû l-Hudhayl does not mean to say that he is the "atoms;" the body as a human body, the locus of the being of whatever "accidents" may define the concrete reality of an individual in time and place, exists through and in the complex

---

37 We have here an almost classical exposition of that legalistic conception of human freedom which is, in a sense, no freedom at all and which, in the words of Berdyaev "humiliates man rather than exalts him".

38 The nature of human existence as abû l-Hudhayl understands it is thus not in any way a perpetual *Sorge* or *Sich-vorweg-schon-sein-in-einer-Welt* (*cf.* Heidegger, *Sein und Zeit*, § 41, pp. 191ff) — a constantly self-determining indeterminate, but rather a self-determining determinate of this to that.

39 *Cf. Maq.*, 257, *Fiṣal* 3, 84, *Milal*, 75; he insists on this in order to maintain the absolute finitude of the totality of created being, both actual and potential, *i.e.*, both as it is contained in God's foreknowledge and as it is and has been realised in the world.

40 Massignon, *Passion*, 480f.

41 *Fiṣal* 5, 65.

of "accidents" which determine the basic materiality (conjunction, etc.) together with those others which determine its specific characteristics, color, etc. Man is the individual in the concrete reality of his material presence in the world [42] and the reality of the "atoms" in their being a substrate for this particular "body" is that of the aggregate of their "accidents." The person, in final analysis, is the totality of his "accidents" at a given moment within their unity of inherence in the body which is itself, in its own reality as a body, a function of a set of defined "accidents." The question then, of the existential unity of the person is one of the oneness of interiority within a complex of "accidents [43]." The problem concerning the ontological oneness of the person arises from the fact that abû l-Hudhayl does not posit or describe a unified and self-totalising act (such as the "soul" in classical and medieval thought) whose being is the reality of the person and through which the body is his living corporeal actuality, but rather he posits the body as an aggregate of undifferentiated "atoms" in which adheres a complex of ontologically distinct "accidents" whose sum within the spatially united substrate constitutes the being of the person.

The question of the ontological oneness of things as bodies, in the spatio-temporal unity of their parts, has been outlined above. So also, as with other created beings, the oneness and density of the human person is, for abû l-Hudhayl, the oneness of the composite totality which is constituted in and by the body; again however, this is not merely an accidental conjunction and juxtaposition in space of the elements of the particulate substrate, but of the living body in its reality as bearing all those permanent "accidents" and functions which adhere in it. In this way man remains always a composite unity; though living and capable of acting, he is not himself the act of his living and his power of acting [44], for such an absolute unity and infinity of self-identity belongs to God alone, the Absolute (*al-Ṣamad*) [45], Who knows and "Whose act of knowing is himself," and Who lives and "Whose life is himself," etc., "like to whom there is none [46]." The act

---

42 *Maq.*, 329.

43 *Cf. infra.*

44 *Cf. supra*, n. 7.

45 On the use of *Ṣamad*, *cf.* for example, the remarks of al-Isfarâ'înî in the preface to his *Tabṣîr* (p.9) ان الصمد هو الذى لا جوف له وهذا يتضمن نفى النهاية; *cf.* also Massignon, *op. cit.*, 645, n. 3 and the references there cited.

46 هو عالم بعلم هو هو وهو قادر بقدرة هي هو, etc., *Maq.*, 165, 484, *et alibi* and *cf.* also *Intiṣâr*, 80 (§70) where *Koran* 42.11 is also cited. The author's treatment of the problem of the *tawḥîd* is remarkably refined and I find it difficult to admit that the discussion of the divine attributes in the early kalâm is no more than "ein mit Schlauheit und Pfiffigkeit geführter Streit um Worte" which was absolutely fruitless (Pretzl, *Attributenlehre*, 35).

and reality of the body in its being a human body is not life and its functions (as it is with Aristotle and the Scholastics); this is not merely that *al-qudra* is distinct from the health and well-being of the body, that the act of perception is distinct from the organs of sense, etc., through the fact that these functions transcend the given states and arrangement of the raw materiality of the body, but rather that those attributes do not belong to it by any intrinsic principle of its being. The elements of his being, though constitutive of the totality in its being what it is, do not properly belong to it in virtue of its being, in itself, that thing which it is, but only through the gratuitous and arbitrary act of the Creator. Although there is a most intimate functional interrelationship between perception, knowledge, thought, and will in the structure of the act and although each and all of these "accidents" is, in its created actuality, founded immediately upon the presence of life in the body, there is no intrinsic basis for their presence in the body. The sole cause and principle of their actual presence in the whole is the will and the action of the Creator. Of and in himself, man does not within himself bear the principle of his own being and the fore-structure of his existence. His presence in the world, through the composite unity of the body, together with the structure of the reality of this presence in terms of the "accidents" which constitute it, are determined from without, there being no formal principle of his being by which he is what he is.

We cannot say, however, simply that the person is nothing more than a mere aggregate of unrelated "accidents" adhering in an assemblage of undifferentiated "atoms." The unity of the living body is not simply that of a merely accidental conglomeration of indivisible parts or a simple, exterior juxtaposition of elements in space. First, it has the ontological unity of its being-created a single, unified body; the union of parts in their constitution of a created body forms, as has been noted, a unity different from that of a simple contiguity of independent parts [47]. Life, again, albeit a distinct "accident," adheres in and infuses (*ḥalla*) the body in the entirety of its "parts" and, insofar as the living body is the reality of the person, it is constitutive of the being of the body in its being the locus of consciousness, will, and the power to act, since these cannot exist apart from the living body [48]. Within the living body, *al-qudra*, in its intimate functional

---

47 *Cf. supra*, ch. II. This abû l-Hudhayl does not state directly but besides its being almost necessary to the consistency of the system, his holding that man cannot make "bodies," though he can cause motion and the "accidents" consequent thereon (*cf. supra*, n. 22) leaves little doubt.

48 That is, *'irâda*, *'ilm* (and so also *'idrâk*), and *qudra* (*istiṭâ'a*) may not exist save in the living, individual body — "may not coexist with death" (*Maq.*, 232 and 313), cf. *supra*, ch. II, n. 6. For comparative purposes it were well to recall at this point that in the Aristotelian and Scholastic systems (in contrast to those of the neo-platonists) the person is the reality of his corporeal existence; "anima est actus totius corporis" (St. Thomas Aquinas, *Comm. in Lib. de Anima*, II, lect, ii, §242) and "non oportet quaerere si ex anima et corpore fit unum... ... forma per se unitur materiae, sicut actus ejus;

relationship of interdependence with perception, knowledge, thought, will, etc., is an "accident" by which the whole body, in all its "parts" is *qâdir mustaṭî'* and so has the free disposition of its own efficacious action. That is, although the particulate or granular quality of the body remains, in the substrate, it is the totality of the parts, as a human individual, which acts [49]; it is the whole, finally, that, in the oneness of its being-created this individual person, is ultimately to be judged "on the last day," in terms of his disposition of himself through his power of self-determination in action. *Al-qudra* is, as we have seen, the power of self-possession and self-determination in moral action of the person in his being "this body which he is" and it is himself, as solely responsible for himself in his action, who is re-created identical with himself in the re-creation of the body at the last judgement.

In the resurrection God will create anew (*marratan 'uḫrà*) the human person in identity with himself as that person which he was created "the first time" (*'awwala marratin*) [50]. The several "accidents" which, together adhering in the unity of the body were that person, are re-created according to the Divine purpose into that corporeal unity whose reality in its unity is the person [51], In sum, there

---

et idem est materiam uniri formae quod materiam esse in actu" (*ibid*, II, *lect.* 1, §234; cf also *Quaestiones disputatae, de Anima, Quaest.* 10f and note the remarks of K. Rahner, *Zur Theologie des Todes* (Freiburg, 1958), pp. 20ff. This position, of course, is quite different from that of abû l-Hudhayl, but the essential materiality of life in the organic unity of the body as the reality of the living creature is common to both positions.

49 *Cf. Maq.*, 330: كان ابو الهذيل يقول ان كل بعض من ابعاض الجسد فاعل على الانفراد ولا انه فاعل مع غيره ولكنه يقول الفاعل هو هذه الابعاض; cf. *Koran* 41.19ff.

50 *Maq.*, 363f.

51 Massignon, speaking of abû l-Hudhayl (*Passion*, 481), states that the resurrection is the simple "reunion of the atoms;" this, however, cannot be the case since it is the "accidents" which constitute the reality of the thing. Though we have no adequate discussion of the topic, this is nevertheless quite clear in his treatment (*Maq.*, 374) of the question of what "accidents" are susceptible of being re-created identical with themselves (of being *mu'âda*). The simple recongregation of a given multitude of undifferentiated and absolutely qualitiless "atoms" cannot reconstitute a "thing" in its being that which it was, no matter what it be, for it is not the mere juxtaposition of parts which is the cause of their being those things which they are. It is for this reason that man cannot himself make a corporeal body or cause life to exist in one (*Maq.*, 403) and even God cannot give him this power (*ibid.*, 378). He cannot, in short, himself be the agent of precisely those "accidents" which make a thing be that thing which it is. It is in this context alone that we can understand the curious statement attributed to abû l-Hudhayl in *'Uṣûl*, 234: كل ماعرف كيفيته من الاعراض فلا يجوز ان يعاد وكل مالا اعرف كيفيته فجائز ان يعاد; that is, only those "accidents" whose nature (*kayfîya*) man does *not* know are capable of being recreated, for man can know and effect only motion and rest (and indirectly by *tawallud* those "accidents" of juxtaposition and separation which are directly consequent upon them — *Maq.*, 311 and 378), *viz.*, those which are by definition not constitutive of the thing in its being that which it is; *cf. supra, nn.* 19 and 21.

is, as it were, in man a disunity of interiority and a unity of exteriority. Within, he is a composite of distinct "accidents" whose unity has its being in their created presence in the body; life itself, the created possibility of the existence of the person in the body is a distinct component of his being and *al-qudra*, which is in a sense a unifying power of self-possession in the body, like life and his very existence, is not properly his own, but like every other element in the structure of his being is grounded in an exteriorly determined act of creation. On the other hand, man is ontologically constituted as one and a unity in the material unity of the body through the transcendent act of creation and God's will which determine his being in being a single, individual person. He is one and identical with himself through a oneness and existence which is not his in any way, out of elements which are not himself.

IV. "ATOM" AND "ACCIDENT" IN THE STRUCTURE OF MATERIAL REALITY

A. *General Remarks*

There can be little question of the "reality" or "concreteness" of "atoms" for abû l-Hudhayl. He says, for example, that a mustardseed (*ḫardala*) could, in theory, be divided (God could divide it) in half and each half in half and so forth until one arrived at an "indivisible part [1]." Again, he holds that these "parts" can exist separately in isolation (*infirâd*) [2] and further states that it would be possible to perceive an "indivisible part" were God to create such an act of perception in us [3].

Created reality can be exhaustively divided into the two categories of "atom" and "accident [4]", but we must be careful as to how we understand the statement that other than the undifferentiated "atoms" everything is "accident." It is especially misleading to take the terms *ǧawhar* ("atom") and *ʿaraḍ* ("accident"), since they have been used by the translators and falâsifa as equivalents of the Greek *οὐσία* and *συμβεβηκός* (Syriac, ܓܕܫܐ), and think of them as "substance" and "accident" as these terms have been used in the Aristotelian tradition [5].

---

1 Maq., 314.

2 *Cf. Maq.*, *ibid* and p. 311: يجوز على الجوهر الواحد الذى لا ينقسم اذا انفرد ما يجوز على الاجسام من الحركة والسكون ومايتولد عنها من الجامعة والمفارقة وسائر ما يتولد عنها.

3 *Maq.*, 315.

4 *Cf. Intiṣâr*, 20f and *infra*, n. 6.

5 There would seem to be some question as to whether abû l-Hudhayl did actually use the term *ǧawhar* or not (*cf.* Pines, *Beiträge*, 3f), while it is certain that he did use the expression *al-ǧuz'u lladî lâ yataǧazza'u/yanqasimu*. At any rate, though the definition of the atom or *ǧawhar* as that which bears "accidents" (*'aʿrâḍ*) is, in a sense, one with that of the Aristotelian *οὐσία* or the scholastic *substantia*, the concepts have little else in common (but *cf. infra*, n. 21). So also, the basic understanding of "accident" in the early kalâm, whatever may be the use of the term *ʿaraḍ* in the translations and the writings of the falâsifa and later mutakallimîn, is entirely different from what it is in the systems of classical antiquity and the latin literature of the middle ages. Fakhry, for example, (*op.cit.*, 34) ignores this fact and, taking *ǧawhar* and *ʿaraḍ* as would be equivalents *in meaning* of "substance" and "accident" in the Aristotelian systems, is unable to understand the position of al-Ǧubbâ'î and, failing therefore to see the coherence of meaning of the terms within their own proper context, ends up by speaking of "fragmentary accounts of substance" (*ibid.*, 35) which underlie the early kalâm.

Certainly for abû l-Hudhayl and most of the early Mu'tazila the basic unit of phenomenal being is body — the bodies (*'ağsâm*) of things. Ultimately, all created being is corporeal, being made up of material bodies with their various "accidents :" qualities, attributes, states, etc. [6]. In this same sense, then, we can quite correctly speak of a basic, implicit materialism in the earlier kalâm [7]. In considering the "atoms" as the basic unit of "things" in their corporeal reality however, we must take care not to lend to them functions which they do not have in the system. Above all, the "atoms" of the early kalâm play no real rôle in the explanation of the physical properties of things; of and in themselves they are altogether qualitiless and absolutely inert, so that we must carefully refrain from seeing in them the atoms of classical systems and from finding in the "materialism" of early Islamic speculation any parallels to modern "materialistic" systems wherein the natures and properties of things are constituted by the nature of matter in and of itself [8]. In the kalâm, the "natures" of things cannot be explained

---

From a purely philological point of view he has overlooked the fact that the principal origins of both the concept and the term (ğawhar = "atom" = οὐσία) are unquestionably stoic (*cf.* references, *infra*, n. 14; Pretzl's attempt to find an Indian origin [*Atomenlehre*, 126ff, *Attributenlehre*, 7f] is not convincing [cf. Pines, *Beiträge*, 122f]). Even this quasi historical equivalence, it should be noted, cannot justify the use of "substance" to translate "*ğawhar*" in the kalâm since, beside the erroneously prejudicial resonance of the term in normal European usage, Muslim authors had no awareness of the common origin of the divergent uses of the word οὐσία in the ancient traditions but rather, in typical Arab fashion, took the usages of the term in the kalâm and the falsafa as simply two distinct meanings (*cf.* for example, the remarks of Taftazânî, *op. cit.*, 62). It is worth noting that the concept οὐσία, as it is understood by Aristotle finds no real equivalent anywhere in the mainstream of Islamic thought (Averroës being marginal), for the concept of the real in its self-subsistent identity with its own being, which is the very center of Aristotle's metaphysics, is reduced by Avicenna and the later mutakallimîn who were influenced by him to a mere "possible essence which when it exists concretely in the world is not in a substrate" (*cf.*, the discussion of Taftazânî, *loc.cit.* and *Šarḥ al-Mawâqif* 5, 10) while the metaphysical system is built chiefly on the notions of "essence" (*ḏât*) and quiddity (*mâhîya*), the possible and the necessary etc.,

6 Cf. Massignon, *Passion*, 549. This is not simply that they are "objets déterminables que le Coran isole" (*ibid.*) but that they are *objects, i.e.*, phenomenal objects of our immediate perception, which have color, movement, etc. It is for this reason that we find the common tendency, when real totalities and their qualities and attributes are in question (as opposed to a discussion of the *ğawâhir* as such) to oppose "accident" and "body" rather than "accident" and "atom". (*Cf.* for example, *Intiṣâr*, 20f, where abû l-Hudhayl is cited, or *Maq.*, 345, where "motion, rest, standing, reclining," etc., are listed as "accidents, not bodies," *et alibi*). Body (*ğism*) is not, strictly, itself an "accident" but rather as a kind of function of " accidents "; *cf. infra.*

7 Massignon, *op.cit.*, 553.

8 Pretzl, prejudiced by non-islamic systems, is determined that an atomism ought to be a "Naturerklärung" (*Atomenlehre*, 122ff) and finding himself unable to deal therefore with the qualitiless inertia of the *ğawâhir* concludes to the primitivity of the kalâm (*cf. supra*, ch. 1). His problem is fundamentally that he wants to find within the composite itself an inherent principle which would explain the *nature* of the thing as that which persists in existence (*op.cit.*, 123). The fact is, however, that the denial of

in terms of their materiality at the level at which this materiality coincides with their atomic substrate.

In brief, the "atom" in the early kalâm is a constitutive element or principle in the *ontological* structure of created beings; it is not meant to give any explanation of the ontic structure or of the physical properties of phenomenal reality [9]. It is important to keep these two things distinct, for the system, as a genuine attempt of the mind to understand itself and the world, is comprehensible only in this way. The birth, "canonisation," and the longevity of this unique type of atomism in Islamic thought is founded precisely in the fact that it did render a truly coherent and intelligible explanation of the ontological or metaphysical structure of being as it was given to an experience paradigmatically moulded in Islam [10].

B. *The "Accidents" as the Reality of the Thing*

All phenomenal being, according to abû l-Hudhayl, is "accident" for the primary objects of our perception are palpable, composite bodies and the "accidents" which inhere in them : configuration, density, color, motion, etc [11]. Most important, bodies themselves, the basic constitutive units of created beings, are themselves in their being bodies, constituted by the "accidents" of composition (*ta'lîf*), conjunction (*iǧtimâ'*), contiguity (*mumâssa*), etc. [12]; that is, extended dimensionality or, more exactly in the terms of the system, the reality of dimension as such or real extension in space, by which a body is constituted as a body, has its reality and its being in the "accidents" of composition and conjunction and is not

---

the existence of any "nature" as an inherent principle of being and activity belonging properly and essentially to created things in and of themselves is a fundamental *apriori* for most of the kalâm; the importance of this assumption for our understanding of the kalâm has been noted above.

9 Arguments against the notion of "prime matter" (*hayûlà*) which ostensibly base themselves on ontic properties of material objects are no more indicative that the *ǧawâhir* are to be taken as physical "atoms" than do the counter arguments (those of Avicenna, for example), which show the same polemic base, indicate that *hayûla* or *materia prima* is not a purely metaphysical concept. Given the very nature of the questions, ontic matter and ontological *materia* or *ǧawâhir* are not always kept completely distinct in the works of many ancient and medieval authors, though it is clear nevertheless that most major writers were quite well aware of the distinction. The same is true of abû l-Hudhayl's speculation about the contiguity of six "atoms" (*Maq.*, 302f and *Šarḥ al-Mawâqif* 6, 294).

10 It is to be noted that even later when the kalâm takes on a much more sophisticated dress, *viz.* the terminology of the falsafa, these basic theses, remain, restated but unchanged in their essential.

11 الاجسام ترى وكذلك الحركات والسكون والالوان والاجتماع والافتراق
والقيام والقعود والاضطجاع وان الانسان يرى الحركة اذا راى الشىء متحركا
(*Maq.*, 361).

12 *Cf. Maq.*, 302f, *et alibi.*

constituted as such simply by the atoms as atoms [13]. The specific dimensionality and configuration which belong to a thing and which determine and constitute the corporeal body whereby the thing is defined as such, is, in this way, the specific and particular "accidents" of length, etc., which arise "in the atoms" through the creation of the "accident" of composition, etc. All further attributes, properties, etc., which may belong to and define a thing are "accidents" which may be said to inhere in the specific body, not however as inhering in the body as such but rather as inhering separately and collectively in the "atoms" which make up the body as that body which it is. The formal reality of things is therefore "accident." The corporality of their materiality as also their every property, attribute, and accident, not only the material density and palpability of the body, but also the reality of its movements, as was noted above, is that of the realisation of an "accident." Al-Ǧuwaynî, therefore is quite correct in saying that the "*mulḥida*", (viz., the falâsifa) call the *ǧawâhir* ("atoms") by the term *hayûlà* (Greek, ὕλη, prime matter) and "accidents" by the term *ṣûra* ("form," Greek ἐιδος) [14]. The "atoms" are in no sense the thing, but rather its reality in being that thing which it is and so also of its being the kind of thing which it is, is the reality of its being a particular aggregate of permanent and transitory "accidents" and its substantiality in existence is the substantiality in existence of the particular aggregate of created "accidents." To be such a thing is to be such a complex of "accidents."

C. *The Atom*

What then is the being of the "indivisible part"? There is no question of its reality within the ontological structure of things as abû l-Hudhayl conceives it, but we must examine the nature of this reality. It is, most simply, by definition a "substrate" (*maḥall*) for the realisation of "accidents" in the world. It is not, as was mentioned above, the "things," for their reality is that of their bodies and all of the "accidents" which adhere in them, permanent and transient. Again, the "atoms" are not, of themselves, in any way real bodies, for body, as such,

---

13 As has been pointed out by Pines (*Beitrage*, 5f) "atoms" are not bodies (*Maq.*, 307); rather "two things neither of which are long are conjoined and there arises a single length" [one long thing or something long] (*Maq.*, 315), body being that which is extended in three dimensions (*ibid.*, and 302f, 306). It is thus that Ibn Taymîya says that body arises as a function of "accidents": الاجسام هى مستلزمة للاعراض (*Muwâfaqa* 1, 186).

14 *'Iršâd*, 23: الجواهر فى اصطلاحهم تسمى الهيولى والاعراض تسمى صورة. Like certain other aspects of the kalâm, this finds an almost exact parallel in the teaching of the Stoa; cf. Max Pohlenz, *die Stoa* (Göttingen, 1948) 1, 66 and also Paul Kraus, *Jabir ibn Hayyan* 2 (Mémoires de l'Institut d'Egypte, 45, Cairo, 1942), 170.

arises as a function of the creation of the particular "accidents" of composition, etc., in a set of "atoms" together with the other "accidents" which qualify its corporeal nature. Ultimately then, the atoms form "points" for the localisation of being, the place or locus of the realisation of "accidents." In the constitution of a body, the simple and unmodified composition of "indivisible parts" forms a kind of skeleton of dimensionality and materiality : a structured framework of the *quanta of potential existence*. Thus, in a very strict sense, the atoms form the *materia prima* of beings in a system in which all being is realised in discrete and discontinuous units in space, — in atomistic quanta of single "things." [15]

The "atom" has no actuality, in one sense, apart from "accidents." Even God, the author holds, cannot strip it completely of them [16]. The minimum "accidents" are those which may inhere in a single isolated "atom" : movement, rest, contiguity, isolation, and *kawn* [17]. Within the categories of the system, these are no more than the basic "accidents" which, in their actuality constitute the reality of the presence of the "atoms" as defined, real points of possible existence in space [18]. They form, we should say, by their inherence therein, the reality of the spatial existence of the "atom" as a possible locus of other "accidents." Considered in itself, the "atoms" form a kind of absolute base for the potentiality of the *maqdûr ʿalayhi* in its existence in the world.

However, the "atom" is an ontological reality distinct in itself, in that it is the stable substrate of a fluctuating multiplicity of momentary and enduring "accidents." Abû l-Hudhayl will not reduce the entire being of things to the "accidents" as do Ibrâhîm al-Naǧǧâr and Ḍirâr b. ʿAmr [19], but insists on the reality of the substrate as the ontological, material base of the being of things. As that which

---

15 *Cf.* Gardet and Anawati, *Introduction*, 325 ("...la vision traditionelle que l'Islam s'est fait du monde : vision essentiellement discontinue."). The "atoms" at this early period were not, probably, considered as mathematical points, however; *cf.* Pines, *Beiträge*, 5f.

16 *Maq*, 311.

17 *Cf. Maq.*, 303, 311, 314f, *et alibi* and also *Maq.*, 325, *Šarḥ al-Mawâqif* 6, 166 (قال الجوهر فى اول زمان حدوثه كائن لا متحرك ولاساكن) and 2, 216 (though abû l-Hudhayl is not here mentioned by name, his position on the matter is cited); regarding *kawn* as an "accident" distinct from movement, rest, etc., and its relationship to these, cf. *supra*, ch. II, 2.

18 It is this difficulty of defining the *ǧawhar* as something (beyond the fact that it has a name) in itself which gave rise to the protracted debate over its nature, which is almost classically stated by al-Šaḥḥâm, abû ʿAbdallâh al-Baṣrî, and Ibn ʿAyyâš, who, in the words of Ǧurǧanî, say that الجوهرية نفس التحيز (*Šarḥ al-Mawâqif* 2, 217; on the latter two *cf.* also abû Rašîd al-Nîsâbûrî, *K. al-Masâ'il*, 12). In the final analysis these basic "accidents", most particularly those of contiguity and isolation, hold here a place analogous to that of the *ṣûra ǧismîya* or *forma corporeitatis* in the system of Avicenna.

19 *Cf. Tabṣîr*, 62f; *Maq.*, 317f and 305f.

persists through successive changes in the creation and annihilation of "accidents," it has a permanence in existence which the great majority of "accidents" do not have. In and of itself however, it cannot be said in any way to have any higher degree of being or greater ontological substantiality than the "accidents," for it too has its being in the same way as the "accidents," through an act of creation, and whatever permanence in existence it has, again, lies in God's causing it to endure, as is also the case with the "accidents." Real things, which make up the world, bodies and their "accidents," exist only as composites of "atoms" and "accidents," within which the constituent parts are all alike dependent in the act of their existence upon God's immediate creation [20]. Neither the *ğawhar* nor the *'araḍ* has the ground of its being strictly in the other. Given the history of the term, we may not therefore, properly apply to *ğawhar* and *'araḍ*, in the kalâm, the terms "substance" and "accident"; to do so is to prejudice, most erroneously, the real meaning of the terms as the authors have used them. Indeed, it is utterly incorrect to say that in the system of abû l-Hudhayl substantial reality lies entirely or primarily in the "atoms." [21].

The being of all things and their substantiality in being lies in their being-created, for this is the ground of the totality of their being. We must, therefore, inquire briefly into the ultimate ontological structure of things in their being-created, if we are to discover and understand the nature of existence and the being of things as it is seen by abû l-Hudhayl.

---

20 *Cf. Maq.*, 363 and *infra*, ch. V.

21 One may, of course, apply the term "substance" to the *ğawâhir* if it be done quite strictly within the limits, say, which Aristotle will allow for the application of the term οὐσία to ὕλη (*n.b.*, *Metaphysics* Z, ch.3, esp. 1029a, 10ff), as indeed the stoics used it.

V. THE BEING OF THE THING

In the period of abû l-Hudhayl the kalâm had not yet taken on the formally abstract vocabulary of Being which is found in the falsafa and the later kalâm, particularly from the beginning of the eleventh century. Here, on the contrary, the vocabulary of Being and Existence is that of creation (*ḫalq*), the initiation of a thing's existence (*al-ibtidâ'*), its continuation in existence (*al-baqâ'*), and the total cessation of its existence (*al-fanâ'*), as has been noted by Pretzl. [1] This fact, however, in no way impeded the incisiveness or the clarity of his thought nor obscured his vision in seeking to uncover and bring to light the ontological structure of created existence, nor, I should insist, indicates any naïveté whatsoever on the part of abû l-Hudhayl or of the other major islamic authors who used the same terminology [2]. Quite on the contrary, in the case of abû l-Hudhayl, despite the limited number of our texts and the biased selection of our sources, one can discern in his handling of the conceptual apparatus which he uses, a highly nuanced precision in his thinking and a remarkable penetration and insight into the most basic problems of metaphysics.

The being of a thing, which is the act by which it exists, is its being-created (*ḫalquhu, takwînuhu*). In a sense we might say that all created existence is event (*ḥâdiṯ, wâqi'*): that it be, i.e., that it "happen," occur in the real world (*ḥadaṯa, waqa'a*) is that it be created (*maḫlûq, muḥdaṯ*) and its reality in being is constituted by and grounded in its being-created. The formal reality of the thing, as was noted above, is the structured complex of its "accidents" so that its reality in being what it is consists in and is grounded in the actuality of the sum of its "accidents," as they adhere in the "substrate." Its substantiality in its being itself is the substantiality of the "accidents" in their inherence in their corporeal substrate. The thing *is* its "accidents" — *is* the complex of "accidents" which is it; its reality in being is the reality of the being of the specific "accidents" in the body as they form the aggregate sum which is the thing. Abû l-Hudhayl says then that from one standpoint "composition" (*ta'lîf*) is "the thing's being created composed," as also "length" is "the thing's being created long" or "color" is "the thing's being created colored [3]." Nothing could be more explicit. In the total complex of

---

1 Pretzl, *Attributenlehre*, 55.

2 *Cf. ibid.*; Pines (*Beiträge*, 19) speaks of an "inadequate conceptual apparatus; "cf. supra, ch.I.

3 *Cf. Maq.*, 366 and 511, *cit, infra*, n. 12.

"accidents" which is, in its aggregate totality, the formal being of the thing, its being such a thing or this kind of thing which it is (the *Sosein*) is constituted by and *is* the actuality of its being-created [4]. The act of being, then, by which it exists, which is its being-created, founds at once the reality of its existence and the plenitude of its being in being that thing which it is. There is no question here of a formal "essence" distinct from the actual existence of the thing; we have not to do with abstract "essences" (*ḏawât*) or quiddities (*mâhiyât*) and their createdness (*maǧʿûlîya*) or intrinsic potentiality (*'imkân ḏâtî*) to be factually present (*wuǧûd*) in the world or to the mind, as in the later kalâm and the falsafa [5].

Prior to its actual existence in the world, a thing simply is not and in itself has no being whatsoever, save in that it is known by God as an object of His omnipotence (i.e., that it is *min maqdûrâtihi*), whose reality in being lies in the realisation of a particular act of His creation. Of and in itself it cannot be said to have any being at all; we cannot say that it potentially *is* or exists itself as a possible, for its being is its being-created and the potentiality of its actual existence consists entirely and unconditionally in God's eternal power-to-create. Prior to the actualisation of the being-created of the thing through the realisation of the act of God's creation, we cannot strictly say the thing potentially exists, *viz.*, that *it*

---

4 *Cf.* Taftazânî, *op. cit.* 87 and the remarks of al-Isfarâ'înî in the margins of the same (p. 89), who complains that in this way abû l-Hudhayl makes the act of creation subsist in the creature (*qâ'im bil-mukawwan*).

5 We keep in mind that the refusal by the early mutakallimîn to speak of "essences" cannot be considered as fortuitous, as was indicated in the preface; the concepts and the terms were "physically" available. This concentration on the concrete thing (*šay'*) and its ontological structure in the order of creation on the part of the early mutakallimîn and their almost total exclusion of any consideration of the logical structure of being, defines and expresses a specific attitude towards reality which most sharply differentiates it from the later writers (*cf.* the remarks of Gardet and Anawati in *Introduction*, 75f, though they do not treat the great muʿtazilî authors of the 11th century). This is not, I should again emphasise, any indication that the problems are not in fact known to the earlier authors, but rather that they took a specific stand on the whole question and analysed the order of being as it was manifested in its appearance within the world defined by that stand. Even in dealing with later authors, particularly in their discussion of their earliest predecessors, one must be quite careful to ascertain whether in using the term *ḏât* ("essence") the author means "essence" as a universal or, as is frequently the case, the individual thing considered in its essential nature in being that thing which it is. The origins of the technical use of the term *ḏât* probably arose out of the common بذاته and as a technical term may well be connected with the Syriac ܢܦܫܐ (*cf.*, بذاته = ܒܢܦܫܗ.) Nevertheless, it should be noted the roots of the distinction in the later kalâm and the falsafa, between *ḏât*/*mâhîya* and *wuǧûd*, are grounded in the kalâm, as has been noted by a number of authors (*cf.* Quadri, *la Philosophie arabe* (Paris, 1947) 102 and reference to Carra de Vaux, Gilson, *l'Etre et l'Essence* (Paris, 1948), 67, Gardet, *la Pensée religeuse d'Avicenne* (Paris, 1951), 45 and reference n. 2) albeit Goichon (*The Philosopher of Being* in *Avicenna Memorial Volume* (Calcutta, 1956) would find its origins in Aristotle and a passage of Plotinus (on which, *cf.* Roland-Gosselin, *de Ente et Essentia* [Paris, 1948], p. xix).

is a potential existent but properly only that there exists God's potentiality or power-to-create. Since abû l-Hudhayl recognises no "essence" or quiddity, there can be no question of potentiality which would reside in a kind of paradigm and which would belong to it as such and whose being would be the being of the "essence" wherefore we should be able to speak of the essential potentiality which belongs to the essence by virtue of its being itself, of itself, that essence which it is in itself, so that consequently the possibility of the thing would be grounded in the thing itself as the possibility of the essence to be realised and defined in the concrete, spatio-temporal existence of the individual.

The Mu'tazila is not infrequently accused of holding just such a position. The thesis, however, which is held by some mu'tazilî authors with a certain variety of detail and diversity of formulation, that the *thing*, prior to its actual, material existence in creation (*al-šay' al-ma'dûm*, *i.e.*, when it is not present in the world) is "something fixed and determined" (*šay' ṯâbit mutaqarrir*) in its createdness, is said to have been introduced into the kalâm by abû Ya'qûb al-Šaḥḥâm, a disciple of abû l-Hudhayl's [6], whereafter it was held by most of the principals of the Baṣra school [7]. The whole debate on this question, as it was later carried on, frequently in a purely abstract terminology of universals and "essences," begins in the question of the status of the particular, individual thing (whether a single *ǧawhar*, "accident," or a composite whole which exists as a single *thing*) as it is known eternally and intended by God as "this particular creature" and in the problem of the identity and self-continuity of the individual human person in the particularity of his unique individuality over the hiatus between death and the resurrection — a particular defined individual as a single person who has been defined in his own existence as the totality of his lived life, whom God will re-create in his total individuality and judge as such "on the last day [8]." Despite the paucity of fragments and the fact that we have no texts ascribed to abû l-Hudhayl which treat directly and explicitly the question of the being of the possible and its status in being prior to its created presence in the material world or, more exactly, its status in its non-presence-in-the-world (*al-'adam*), in that it is that thing which is to be created (*creandum*) itself that which it shall be, we can nevertheless glean from what little information is given in the sources and out of the general consistency of the system a reasonably clear conception

---

6 *Cf. Nihâya*, 150 and *Milal*, 76.

7 *Cf.* the list in Râzî's *Muḥaṣṣal*, 37f.

8 Among others, *cf.* the remarks of Râzî in *K. al-'Arba'în*, 63 and generally the whole chapter. This is a complex problem whose treatment is far from simplistic in those writers who adhere to the thesis and the position of each must be studied in the contextual matrix of the particular system. *Cf.* also the following note.

of how he understood the possibility of existence of that which is not. The possibility of the existence, as the potentiality of a thing which materially exists in the world to continued existence and alteration has already been outlined in part above. Things, according to abû l-Hudhayl, discrete and individual, which exist, can be said to *be* and to have *their* existence only in the reality of their being themselves in themselves and identical with themselves in the actuality of their being-created, but, as was pointed out above, this, insofar as it is a real possibility, resides solely and unconditionally in God's power of creation. We cannot properly say that the thing *is* potentially existent in the state of its non-presence-in-the-world, but only that God's potentiality to create what He knows as the object of His power-to-create *is* and that this power, as such, is constitutive of itself in its reality and so also of the possibility of its objects. The objects, in themselves, have no being and are not themselves in themselves their own potentiality. A thing can itself be said to *be* only in its being a created being (*šay' maḫlûq*) in its being-created; *i.e.*, it exists itself in being, in itself, that thing which it is, only in the actuality of the realised act of its being-created (*ḫalquhu*). Considered in itself it has no being at all save in the created existence of the material composite which takes place (*ḥadaṯa*) in the concrete dimensions of time and place. [9] In this way then, a thing's being, in its being

---

[9] Cf. Râzî, *Muḥaṣṣal*, 34. The very statement of abû l-Hudhayl that "color" is the "thing's being created colored" etc., (*cf. infra*) is indicative. Nader, however (*Système*, 130) says that abû l-Hudhayl, al-Ka'bî and his disciples of the Baghdad school, held that "le néant possible d'exister" was something stable and fixed, etc. His citations to the *Šarḥ al-Mawâqif* I could not check, having no access to the edition from which he draws his citations (*viz.*, that of Constantinople, 1286); on the other hand, Ǧurǧânî does quite clearly and explicitly say in this work (ed. Cairo, 1325, vol. 2 p., 190) that *except for* abû l-Hudhayl, abû l-Husayn al-Baṣrî, and al-Ka'bî and his disciples of the Baghdad school, the Mu'tazila held that the thing, prior to its existence (*i.e.*, considered as a possible in the state of its non-existence as its non-presence-in-the-world), is something fixed and determined, etc.; in this he follows the same statement (though without reference to al-Ka'bî and his followers) in the *Nihâya* of Šahrastânî (*loc.cit.*). (Abû l-Ḥusayn Muḥammad b. 'Alî al-Basrî was a disciple of the Qâḍî 'Abd al-Ǧabbâr, who broke with his master on this point; *cf.* Râzî, *I'tiqâdât*, 45 and also his *K. al-'Arba'în*, 53f and 59, Ibn al-Murtaḍà, *Ṭabaqât al-Mu'tazila*, [ed. S. Diwald-Wilzer, Wiesbaden, 1961] 118f. *Milal*, 130f and Ǧurǧânî, *op.cit.*, 2, 212f, who notes that his position on this point was similar to that of the Aš'arites) The habit common to many authors of ascribing, without qualification, the position of al-Balḫî to the Mu'tazila *in toto*, even though a number of mu'tazilî writers (besides those mentioned, *e.g.*, Hišâm al-Fuwaṭî — *cf. Maq.*, 158 and *Fiṣal* 5, 42) did not adhere to such a thesis, would arise from polemical considerations and from the fact that by the late 11th century the only surviving mu'tazilî schools were those of abû Hâšim and abû l-Ḥusayn al-Baṣrî, the latter in all probability being of little importance; as for our chief earlier sources, abû l-Ḥusayn, given the time of his activity, would hardly have been known to al-Baġdâdî, Ibn Ḥazm, or al-Isfarâ'înî.

It should be noted that the whole problem, especially insofar as one is concerned with the interpretation of the statements of earlier writers, is rendered difficult in great part because of the polemical way in which it is treated by many of our "orthodox" sources; it is set forth, for example, in the *Nihâya*

what it is, is altogether constituted by and grounded in the fact *that it is*, viz., the reality of its being-created. Apart from the terminology and considering the thing (*ens*) only in the concrete reality of its being itself in its being-created, we find in abû l-Hudhayl's conception of the existent thing an understanding analogous to the Aristotelian οὐσία, in that the thing's being what it is (τὸ τί ἐστι) is one with the fact it is (ὅτι ἐστι, τὸ εἶναι) [10]. The reality of the thing is the being-created of the "accidents" as they are the thing in their inherence in the "substrate," and its formal reality, in being that thing which it is, is not in any way separable from the reality of its spatio-temporal existence in being-created.

It should be said in passing that this restriction of the being and reality of the thing to its being and reality as it exists concretely in the world is not due to any inadequacy in the language and the terminology available to the author, i.e., to the fact that the terms for being and existence are "creation," "perdurance in existence," etc., for the problem of the reality and being of a thing as it is known by God as a possible or as a determined object of His power is discussed with considerable refinement by other authors using the same terminology [11]. The thing however, is not the ground of its own existence. This is not simply that the thing's being what it is is distinct from the fact that it actually exists; this is a fundamentally logical distinction with which abû l-Hudhayl does not concern himself. On the contrary, while it is identical with its being as its being-created (*ḫalq*), "that act of creation which is the thing's being-created that which it is" is itself "created" (*maḫlûq*) [12]. Being-created (*ḫalq*) is other than its ground

---

(150ff) or the *K. al-'Arba'in* (*loc. cit.*) in the form of a quasi debate in which the thesis that the "*šay' ma'dûm*" is "something" i.e., a being, is expounded in its most extreme form, *viz.*, as implying the eternity of "essences" and so of "things" in themselves, since it was precisely this which the opponents of the thesis felt to be the fundamental danger inherent in it. In his failure to study the texts carefully and to take all this into consideration, Nader completely misinterprets the facts (*Système*, 135) and contrary to all the evidence ends up by saying "n'est pas là un subterfuge auquel ont eu recours les mu'tazila pour dissimuler leur croyance à l'étérnité du monde... ?" ! Ğurğânî, though expressing himself in abstract terms which are basically foreign to the earlier kalâm, quite correctly notes in his discussion of the "createdness of quiddities" that the argument in this subject between the Mu'tazila and the 'Ašâ'ira is purely terminological (*cf. Šarḥ al-Mawâqif* 2,213 and 3, 40ff [*maqṣad* 6 : الماهيات الممكنة هل هي مجعولة], esp., 48ff; *cf.* also the remarks of Siyâlkûtî, *ibid.*, 2, 189 and 3, 46f) and carefully refers in his discussion to "the opinion ascribed to the Mu'tazila" (*ibid.*, 3, 50; this remark is picked up and discussed by Siyâlkûtî, *ibid.*, 3. 45 and also at 2, 198).

10 *Cf.* generally, Gilson, *l'Etre et l'Essence*, 46ff.

11 *Cf.*, for example, *Maq.*, 158f, *et alibi.*

12 قال ابو الهذيل الخلق الذى هو تاليف والذى هو لون والذى هو طول وخلق الله سبحانه للشىء مؤلفا الذى (*Mag.*, 366); والذى هو كذا مخلوق فى الحقيقة هو تاليف وخلقه للشىء ملونا الذى هو لون وخلقه للشىء طويلا الذى هو طول مخلوق فى الحقيقة *ibid.*, 511. *cf.* also the same statement, attributed to the 'aṣḥâb abî l-Hudhayl, *ibid.*, 189f.

which is the act of creation (*ḫalq*)! Abû l-Hudhayl has not simply taken the term *al-ḫalq* twice, once as active and once as passive, to play a game with the word but has analysed, rather, the density of that nexus which is most eloquently expressed in the absoluteness of the *maṣdar* [13], *viz.*, that point where the being of the thing as a being-created is the realisation of the act of creation. The ground of the thing's reality in its being-created and the actuality of its existence is the act of creation (*ḫalq*), but "the creation of a thing is other than the thing [14]." On the one hand, thus, it is one with the fullness of its own being, insofar as this is the reality of its being-created; that is, it is identical in its being what it is with the reality of its own existence, in that this act of existence is its being-created, while on the other hand, its being-created, as created is not its own self-sufficient and self-subsistent ground.

Viewed from this standpoint, whether in the initiation of its existence (*ibtidâ'uhu*), its continuance in existence (*baqâ'uhu*), or its passing totally out of existence (*fanâ'uhu*), the being of a thing, as the ground of its actuality, is the realisation of the act of the agent (*fâ'il qâdir*) [15] or Creator and so is distinct from it. "The initiation of existence is other than the thing initiated [16]" and "the perdurance of a thing in existence is other than that which perdures [17]". "In this way then, the ground of the existence of the thing in the act of its existence in the world is, insofar as it "belongs" to the agent and is the act of the Creator, distinct from the thing which exists, present in the world [18]. The creation which is the being-

---

13 Throughout this discussion it must be carefully borne in mind that the *maṣdar* or infinitive indicates, of itself, the event or act in a most stark and absolute way, without any direct reference to either agent or object (and so without being of itself either active or passive) or any notion of time relative to the speaker (*cf.* generally the remarks of Miskawayh in *al-Kitâb* [ed. Derenbourg, Paris, 1881], 79f). This semantic compactness of absoluteness of the form is very important. If, indeed, the beginnings of the kalâm represent an epochal moment in the history of human thought, there can be little doubt that certain elements of the linguistic structure of Arabic, such as the density of the *maṣdar*, played an important rôle therein. One must beware of pushing such a thesis too far, but on the other hand, there can be little question but that had the linguistic structure been other than it was, certain facts of the problems treated would perforce have been differently seen, stated, and treated. Linguistic differentiation is an irreducible source of variety and fecundity in the history of speculative thought and the fruitfulness of the work of the early mutakallimîn both for Islam and eventually, through the great falâsifa, for the West, lay thus in part in some of the unique qualities of the Arabic language and in what Heidegger has called "die Nennkraft des Wortes" (*Holzwege*[3] [Frankfurt a/M., 1957], 35); *cf.* also the remarks of Gilson, *op. cit.*, 11.

14 خلق الشىء غيره *Maq.*, 366.

15 *Cf.* supra on the thing as *al-maqdûr 'alayhi.*

16 كان ثبت الابتداء غير المبتدا *Maq,.* 364.

17 البقاء غير الباقي, *Maq.*, 366.

18 That is, we must take "the thing which perdures" (*al-bâqî*) or "the thing created" (= "*that which results from*" the act of creation [*mâ waqa'a 'an al-qawl*]) as the thing in its being "this thing which it is."

created of the thing, in its being that thing, and which is "strictly speaking created" (*fî l-ḥaqîqati maḫlûq*) is founded in ("results from" — *waqaʿa ʿan*) [19] a simultaneous act of creation (*ḫalq*) [20] which "can only metaphorically be termed created [21]." For abû l-Hudhayl the being of a thing (*ḫalquhu*), in the reality of its existence in the world, is totally grounded in the act of God's will (*'irâda*) and in the act of creation which is "His saying 'be' (*kun*)" [22], as also its continuance in existence lies in God's saying "endure" (*ibqa*) and its passing out of existence in His saying "cease to exist" (*ifna*) [23]. "The thing created is that which results from God's saying 'be'." The ground of its being as the act of creation which is this "Be", because of its association with the reality, in time, of the thing which exists through, it can thus metaphorically be said to "become" and even to be created, but in itself, it is distinct from the thing and the temporality and spatiality of the world. As God's act of willing the thing and commanding it to *be*, the act of existence is strictly speaking uncreated [24] and forms no part of the created world; it is immaterial, "not in any place" (*lâ fî makân*) [25]. The author does not insist that the act of existence which is God's creative act (*al-ḫalq*, *al-baqâ'*, etc.) does not "occur" (*ḥadaṯa*) or have its actuality "in a place" or in a substrate (*maḥall*) — *viz.*, in the thing — merely in order to avoid having "an accident inhere in an accident" as has been suggested [26]. To exist in space is to inhere in

---

19 كل ذلك مخلوق فى الحقيقة (*Maq.*, 541) معنى مخلوق انه وقع عن ارادة من الله وهو واقع عن قول وارادة (*ibid.*, 366), *cf also ibid.*, 511.

20 والخلق مع المخلوق فى حاله *Maq.*, 363.

21 *Cf. Maq.*, 366 and 511.

22 خلق الله للشيء [الذى] هو تكوينه بعد ان لم يكن هو غيره وهو ارادته وقوله له كن ... وابتداء الله الشيء بعد ان لم يكن هو خلقه له وهو غيره (*Maq.*, 363f.); cf. also *ibid.*, 541 : انه واقع عن ارادة من الله وقوله له كن.

23 والبقاء غير الباقى والفناء غير الفانى والبقاء قول الله عز وجل للشيء ابق والفناء قوله افن *Maq.*, 366, *cf.* also *Farq*, 76, §5 and ان البقاء هو قول الله عز وجل للشيء ابقه وكذلك فى بقاء الجسم وفى بقاء كل ما يبقى من الاعراض *Maq.*, 359.

24 The term *ḥâdit* is used of it, for example, in *Farq*, *loc. cit.* and *'Uṣûl*, 51 and 106 (*cf.* also *Šarḥ al-Mawâqif* 5, 8f); *i.e.*, as being simultaneous with the thing it is not strictly *qadîm*, although it remains nevertheless strictly uncreated : ليس بمخلوق فى الحقيقة وانما يقال له مخلوق فى المجاز (*Maq.*, 510f)

25 *Maq.*, 363; *cf.* also *ibid.*, 369 and 189f and *Farq*, 76, *'Uṣûl*, 106. The use of the term *ʿaraḍ* (*Maq.*, 369) for this act of God's Will and His act of creation, if it was actually used by abû l-Hudhayl alongside *ḥâdiṯ* (*ibid.*, *cf.* also *supra*) is probably due in part to the lack of any other category in which to put it, since all being, other than that of God Himself, is ex-haustively divided by *ʿaraḍ* and *ǧawhar* (cf. Čelebî in *Šarḥ al-Mawâqif* 4, 99).

26 Cf. Pines, *Beiträge*, 25; on the question of the inherence of an "accident" in an "accident", *cf.* also *supra*.

a substrate (*ğism, maḥall, ğawhar*, etc.) and is consequently to be a creature. To say that the act was part of or inhered in the creature would be to involve one's self in the infinite regression of Muʿammar's "*maʿânî*" or to make the creature identical with the ultimate ground of its own being [27], while to make it inhere in some substrate of its own, *i.e.*, to give it an existence of its own as a material creature would make no sense at all [28]. In sum, to adapt a statement of Heidegger's "Sein kann nicht *sein*. Würde es sein bliebe es nicht mehr sein, sondern wäre ein Seiendes [29]." The ultimate ground of being cannot belong to the creature and cannot itself be created.

From one standpoint then, that the thing exist is identical with its being that particular, defined thing which it is and as such, we can say that the thing is itself subsistent in its own being; it is itself the being-created which is it. This act of existence, however, which is the reality of its being-created cannot be identical with the ultimate ground of its being, precisely insofar as it is the fullness of the thing in the concreteness of its being created. In itself, the thing is a being-created and this being constitutes its reality in the fullest content of its being. Though from one standpoint it is thus subsistent in its own being, it is, on the other hand, altogether contingent and dependent upon the act of creation which is the ultimate ground of its being. Again, we must keep in mind that the question here is not of the contingency of an "essence" in its real presence in the world, but of the being which is the reality of the thing in being, the *esse* which is the *perfectio entis*. Thus also, in itself and of itself, though subsistent in the world in its being-created, it remains an aggregate of "accidents" whose unity in being consists in the spatial conjunction of its parts (*'ağzâ'* or *ğawâhir*) or its body, together in isolation from other things. Considered, however in the act which created the juxtaposition and composition in space, which is the unity of the thing and the creation in the corporeal composite of all the other "accidents" which inhere in it, its unity is complete and perfect in its being that thing which it is;

---

[27]   It is precisely this of which al-Taftazânî complains (*op. cit. supra*, n. 4) concerning abû l-Hudhayl's statement that the being-created of the thing is its being that which it is, as is noted by ʿIsâmuddîn al-Isfarâ'înî (*cit. ibid.*)

[28]   Fakhry seems not to have understood this completely when he says (*op. cit.*, 47) that "both abû l-Hudhayl and al-Jubbâ'î... further maintained the exceptional thesis that God could create an accident in no substratum..." He does note (*ibid.*) that such a thesis "was doubtless an expedient for interpreting their theological notion of the creation and the annihilation of the universe," but failed to grasp the real sense of this "expediency" having taken the statement of *Farq*, 76 at face value without analysing its meaning in terms of abû l-Hudhayl's context or taking into account the polemical nature of al-Baġdâdî's account.

[29]   *Kants These über das Sein* (Frankfurt a/M., 1963), 35.

its ontological density, in the ground of its existence, in being itself the totality of that which it is, is that of a true unity.

In the same way, as was pointed out above, the thing cannot strictly be said to be its own potentiality. Its potentiality resides rather in the potentiality (*qudra*) of the source of its being. Of and in itself it has not, strictly speaking, either its own actuality in existence or its own potentiality but is ever a creature subject to the power of its creator — *maḫlûq maqdûr 'alayhi.*

To sum up then, the thing is itself subsistent in its own being, which is the principle of the total content of its being that thing which it is in the actuality of its being, but this being is a being-created which is altogether contingent upon an act of creation which is uncreated and totally independent of the thing and of any worldly contingency. In the scholastic terminology, it is from one aspect an *ens subsistens*, whose *esse* is the principle of its total reality (*perfectio essendi*), but its *esse*, as the act of that reality which it is, being an *esse creatum* is not *per se subsistens* but is itself grounded in an uncreated act which is *per se subsistens, viz.*, God's Will and Creative Command. We have thus in abû l-Hudhayl an understanding of the ontology of the created thing (the *ens creatum* and its *esse creatum*) which is in some ways more akin to St. Thomas' understanding of the relation between *esse* and *essentia* than to Avicenna's conception which is one of the difference rather between *quidditas* and *existentia* [30]. For abû l-Hudhayl the question is not that of the mere factual state of being present in the world or in the mind as this state constitutes the factic mode of existence of a determined thing but rather of the ontological structure of reality at a far more basic level.

---

30 On this question generally and the difference between the two points of view (which are not by necessity mutually exclusive) *cf.* the excellent discussion of E. Coreth, *die Metaphysik*² (Innsbruck, 1964) §25, pp. 180ff, esp. *Zusatz* 1 pp. 187ff, where he treats of the difference between the positions of St. Thomas and Suarez.

Drukkerij Orientaliste, p.v.b.a., Leuven (België).